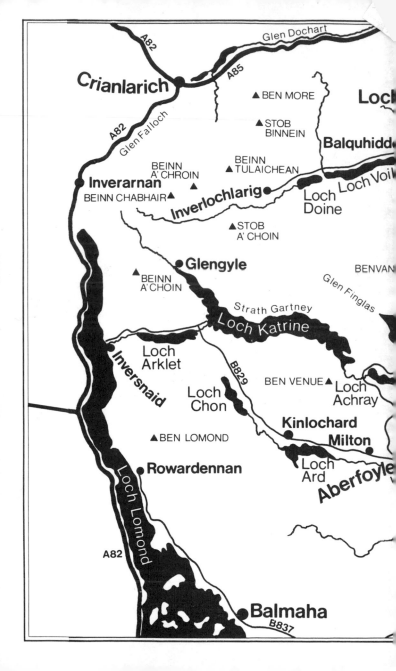

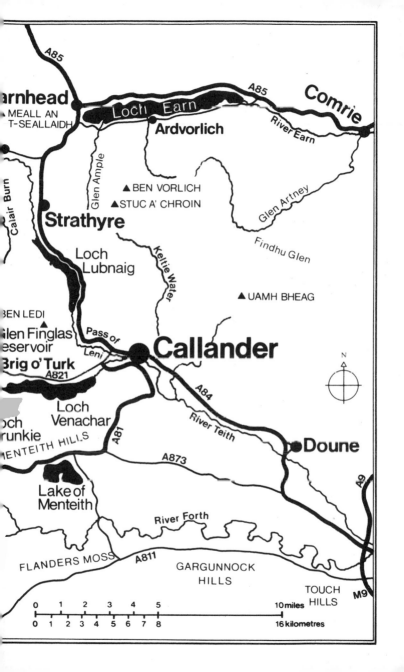

WALKS
IN THE
TROSSACHS
&ROB ROY COUNTRY

Rennie McOwan

THE SAINT ANDREW PRESS
EDINBURGH

First published in 1983 by
THE SAINT ANDREW PRESS
121 George Street, Edinburgh EH2 4YN

Copyright © Rennie McOwan, 1983

ISBN 0 7152 0563 3

Reprinted 1986

Printed and bound in Great Britain by
Thomson Litho Ltd, East Kilbride, Scotland

For the Children of the Mist—past and present

We are the children of the hills and of the mists—
The hills make no change, the mists are always coming
back, and the deer is in the corrie yet.

Neil Munro, *Doom Castle* (Blackwood, Edinburgh)

Cover photograph of the Lake of Menteith
by K. J. H. Mackay
Drawings by John MacKay
Map by Fenella Duncan

Contents

Acknowledgements

Grateful thanks are due to Duncan MacLaren who patiently corrected my Gaelic, to Ian Fraser of the School of Scottish Studies for help with many place-names, to Mrs Elizabeth Beauchamp for expert advice about Balquhidder, to the Scottish Landowners' Federation and to Dr K. J. H. Mackay for helpful comments. Any mistakes are my own.

Thanks, too, to good hill companions, my wife Agnes and my children, Lesley, Michael, Tom and Niall, to Jim Crumley, Alastair McGowan, Alastair Chalmers, Colin Bayes (and Hannah Bayes, aged three, who went to the top of Uamh Bheag and Cruachan Hill on foot and 'in' a rucksack).

Foreword

The Trossachs country is only twenty-five miles north of Glasgow, yet is legendary land. Here were set great tales from Scotland's past. Whether tales from the clans' records, or of poetic narratives like Scott's, or of folklore and prehistory, they all share in the romance of a fabled hill-scene. For the hills and crags are moated like castles by deep-set lochs, which stretch long and wide around wooded lower slopes. The woodlands being largely oak, birch, hazel and beech, they light the land in spring and fire it in autumn. In winter, their bare tops haze the glens like brume, lending height to the snow-peaks.

In former days, when the Trossachs was roadless and bridgeless, it became a natural fortress held by a strong, Highland population. It bred its own adventurous life. As Rennie McOwan notes, it is to this day known as 'the Rob Roy country'—and Rob in his own lifetime brought it first to nation-wide attention. Its discovery by the nineteenth-century travellers and poets gave its landscape a literary fame that still fell short of the honour due. Gradually the Trossachs was opened up. Access is now for all. But the motorist will delude himself should he think that the Trossachs can be known from the roadside, for there is only one way to know land, and that is to walk in it. It cannot otherwise be intimately seen, or fully enjoyed. To walk is to know, and to know is to love this land. Rennie McOwan's book gives to us all a real service. He is one man who does know his subject fully. He can lead us where we would want to go. The Trossachs and Loch Lomondside are threaded by paths and tracks and hidden ways, which would take us years to find out without him. Yet, while guiding us, he does so with the discretion of the devotee, never depriving us of the opportunity that he wants us to share—the chance to explore on our own, to discover for ourselves, and so to enter into a real sense of possession.

W. H. Murray

Introduction

The area covered by this book is one of great beauty. It is a tamed landscape from past centuries with lochs now reservoirs, unsightly bulldozed 'roads' on hillsides, pylons in the glens, roads through the passes, and much forestry planting.

Nevertheless, it is still possible to find hills and glens very much as they were in the days of the red MacGregors and there are immense rewards for the stravaiger (wanderer) and the mountaineer.

The boundaries of this book are Balquhidder (pronounced Balwhidder) of the Braes and Loch Earn to the north, and the Loch Earn Hills and Glen Artney to the east. The western boundary is the east shore of Loch Lomond, and the towns of Callander and Aberfoyle mark the south.

In past centuries the name Trossachs was only applied to the area around Ben Venue, the south end of Loch Katrine and Loch Achray, but popular modern usage has widened it to include other hills and lochs between there and Aberfoyle and Callander.

There is debate about the meaning of the name Trossachs, but *Na Troiseachan*, the cross-hills, has been suggested. The 'bristly ground' has also been mooted and that is certainly appropriate.

INTRODUCTION

Rob Roy MacGregor (1671–1734) is one of Scotland's great folk-heroes. He is the subject of much myth, but the truth is greater than the legend.

He was born at Glen Gyle, Loch Katrine, emerged as an energetic and talented leader and at one stage was the *de facto* chief of a branch of his clan. A brilliant organiser and tactician, he indulged in the accepted pastime of cattle reiving (stealing). At the same time he gained a reputation for fair and honest dealing as a cattle-dealer, built up a large business and acquired land at Inversnaid and Craigrostan. However, he was ruined by his chief drover absconding with his funds. He set out to honour his debts but powerful enemies such as the Duke of Montrose and the hatchetman, Graham of Killearn, seized the opportunity to persecute him and take his lands, and he was outlawed. In the 1715 Rising he fought with the Jacobites and for most of his life smote his adversaries. On at least three occasions he was arrested and his escapes became legendary. He stole from the rich and protected the poor.

Rob Roy successfully outwitted two dukes and the British Army and, surprisingly, died peacefully in his bed at Inverlochlarig, Balquhidder.

There is no space to say any more, but do read W. H. Murray's book, *Rob Roy MacGregor* (Richard Drew, Glasgow). It is the definitive work and indispensable reading for a visit to this area.

So, too, is Sir Walter Scott's epic poem *The Lady of the Lake*, published in 1810. The poem's popularity gave the Trossachs area a tourism boost which has continued to this day. Sir Walter (1771–1832) made many visits to this area and drew heavily on his experiences for novels like *Waverley, Rob Roy* and *The Legend of Montrose.* Most large bookshops carry volumes of Scott poetry but some second-hand versions of *The Lady of the Lake*, with notes, are the best.

Scott's first introduction to the scenery of *The Lady of the Lake* came about 1790 when, as an apprentice in his father's law office, he made an expedition to Balquhidder to execute a judgement against refractory tenants of Stewart of Appin, probably MacLarens of Invernenty. He had an escort of six soldiers under a sergeant who knew the district well and from this man he heard tales of Rob Roy.

In 1793, now an advocate, he visited Highland friends and one of the places he stayed at many times was Cambusmore House, south-east of Callander. The young laird, a Buchanan, was his guide on some of the 'merry excursions' mentioned in the notes to *The Lady of the Lake.*

When he thought of writing a romantic narrative poem about Highland and royal loves and war he was already famous as the author of *The Lay of the Last Minstrel* and *Marmion.* He also extensively studied the countryside around Callander, Aberfoyle and Loch Lomond.

The poem is out of fashion nowadays but it made this district world famous and gave a decisive impetus to the development of Highland tourism.

Sir John Sinclair wrote that it was *The Lady of the Lake* that sent 297 carriages to Loch Katrine in six months when only a fifth of that number had previously gone in a year.

INTRODUCTION

Few poems in any language have been more widely read and at one time it was prescribed reading in schools.

The boundaries of this book are, to some extent, subjective. The area is a natural catchment one and I have included some passes leading out of it. The walks range from short strolls for the family and the dog, full hill-walking expeditions, way-marked forest trails and lonely peaks. Take your pick.

The text is as accurate as one can humanly make it at the time of going to press, but if you come across a fence that was not there before or find a bridge or stile has vanished please do not get too irate. There have been many such changes over the years, sometimes in a 24-hour span.

You are walking in the honoured tradition of many men and women who loved this area, who found a wilder country than we do now, and who were hardy and resilient. There has to be freedom, adventure and the unexpected in the outdoors and minor snags should be treated in that spirit.

You are also now walking in an area of modern hill-farming, forestry and tourism facilities and these factors must also be understood and appreciated.

Most of the place-names are Gaelic in origin although the language has virtually vanished as a spoken tongue from this area.

The ancient Picts (Caledonians) lived here in the years before they were absorbed by the Scots from Ireland who eventually gave their name to the nation we now call Scotland (A.D. 843).

Here, too, the Celtic saints brought Christianity from Ireland in the sixth century and from southern Scotland in the fifth century. They were men of peace

4

who walked, sailed or rode to turbulent kingdoms and who left their mark in place-names on the map of Scotland.

The Romans probed northwards from what is now England but were not able totally to subdue the tribes and built forts at Bochastle (at the foot of Ben Ledi), at the Lake of Menteith and at Comrie.

The hills and glens were also a haven for Scotland's most famous king, Robert Bruce, who conducted guerrilla warfare here during the fourteenth-century Scottish Wars of Independence which successfully maintained Scotland's status as a nation.

From here, too, MacGregors, MacLarens, Campbells, Stewarts, Fergusons and Grahams travelled to take part in the seventeenth-century Scottish Wars of the Covenant (the Scottish-end of what is popularly known in England as the Roundheads and Cavaliers war) and in the 1715 and 1745 Jacobite Risings, and in other power clashes.

The large Highland cattle drives of the eighteenth and nineteenth centuries also passed through part of the area on their way to the big fairs at Falkirk and Crieff, the roast beef of old England on its way south from Scotland.

The word blackmail came from these glens—black for the old Highland cattle (the shaggy brown types seen today are a nineteenth-century crossbreed) and mail from an old Scots word for rent.

In effect, the MacGregors and others said to the Lowland lairds or landowners—pay us cash and we won't steal your cattle and we won't let anyone else do so either. This is not as bad as it sounds as it was a kind of primitive policing and evolved into bodies of

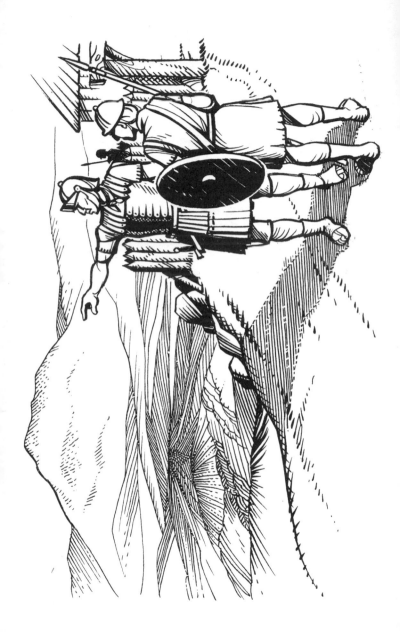

law-and-order government-sponsored militia called Watches.

In the nineteenth century and later, the tourists and the literati came to the Trossachs: Sir Walter, Boswell and Johnson, Coleridge and Ruskin, Keats, the Wordsworths, Carlyle, A. J. Cronin, Robert Louis Stevenson, James Hogg, Nathaniel Hawthorne, Gerard Manley Hopkins and others.

But perhaps, above all, the most poignant relics of the past are the remains of old clan townships, now buried by trees, or the foundations of shielings in fertile corners of now empty glens and moors, monuments to the Gaelic people who took their herds there in the spring and summer months.

Their life was often precarious and hard, but in addition to poetry and songs of wars and heroes they also produced music and verse of great beauty and sensitivity about human relationships and love of one's native place.

They were hardy hillmen and women and walked long distances as a normal part of human activity.

The area is a magnificent heritage of shining lochs, deep woods, blue hills and green glens. Happy stravaiging!

EQUIPMENT

For woodland, way-marked walks of short length in summer no more special clothing is required than for a short walk in the park. The same is true of informal and short-length strolling in woods.

The probing Romans established temporary forts to try and control the Highland passes.

INTRODUCTION

Long woodland trails require stout shoes or boots, warm and windproof clothing, and sufficient food and drink for the day. It is better to have too many clothes and remove some, rather than to have too few and shiver.

If snow is on the hills no inexperienced person should be there unless adequately clad and equipped and accompanied by experienced companions.

Scottish hill weather in spring and winter can be ferociously cold and wild, with temperatures similar to Arctic Norway, wind-levels that can knock a man off his feet and stupefy the senses and a raw cold that can easily bring on exposure to the ill-prepared.

In spring there can be late snowfalls and in summer there can be much rain. Pleasant temperatures low down do not mean that that is the situation on high ground.

For a day's outing in summer through a pass, or across moors, or on to hills the walker should have:

Boots or stout shoes.

Long, warm trousers.

Anorak.

Cagoule-style outer jacket or 'coat', with hood.

Food and drink for the day, including a reserve.

Adequate rucksack and a map, compass and whistle.

Underclothing and jerseys are a matter of personal taste but unless you are very lucky with a heatwave, shorts and jeans are inadvisable although frequently worn. Again, it is easier to strip than to be caught out.

Gaiters are also a useful item, and a plastic survival bag is also carried by many. Plasters for possible blisters and spare laces are a help.

INTRODUCTION

In winter, a balaclava helmet, warm underwear of a thermal or 'long-John' type, mitts of an approved thick-wool type, spare jerseys, overtrousers, a *torch* and scarf, are essential in addition to the other items listed above.

If walking on hills in the winter an ice-axe is a must, and so is the ability to use it. Crampons often need to be donned for high-level winter walking.

PRECAUTIONS

A person who hill-walks all year round in Scotland is not a walker, or rambler, but a mountaineer. Stick to routes within your capabilities. Three miles an hour *on the flat* is an average walking pace, and at least half an hour or more should be allowed for each thousand feet of ascent.

Solitary wandering in winter is unwise except for the very experienced. No one likes restrictions and the oft-repeated dictum of never-go-alone is frequently challenged with reason by those who argue that there are times when personal solitude or just one close companion is a desirable situation.

One of the main attractions of going to the hills, glens and moors is freedom from direction, restriction and pressure. Each person has to decide to what extent he or she balances that with possible trouble and inconvenience for others if things go wrong. It is always a puzzle that lone hill-walkers are criticised and lone yatchsmen are knighted.

In many cases it is wise to leave a note with friends about your route and estimated time of return.

The midge (gnat) is a problem in summer, a tiny insect with an infuriating bite which is particularly virulent in humid weather, by lochsides, near or in trees and on the lower moors. It can be devastating in the evenings.

Anti-midge cream or lotion has greatly improved in recent years. Check with the local chemist. The writer finds Coghlan's clear lotion insect repellant effective, but it is a matter of personal choice.

Sometimes there is no antidote except to pray for a breeze or head for the pub.

Adders, Scotland's only poisonous snake, are retiring creatures and have an undeservedly notorious reputation. They are very rarely seen and want to be left alone. If you should by chance be bitten, a *very* rare occurrence, head speedily for the nearest medical help. Adders are there as a fact, but there are also people around who are lifetime hill gangrels (wanderers) and who have never seen one.

Most of the main walks and routes in the catchment area are included in this book. Some corners have been left out because it is legitimate for people to keep knowledge of some attractive places to themselves as far as that is humanly possible. Some walks, sections of which have become so eroded by unbearable boot-pressure, have also been left out in a bid to help the ground recover. Some others, similarly affected, are so well-known that they could not be ignored, but I have told the reader of the condition of that walk and it is up to each person to make a choice about going there or not. One or two have been omitted for space reasons. The basic idea is to give main routes and a general flavour.

Each person will have his or her favourite season, but perhaps the most poignant times are in May when spring comes late to the Highlands, with a mist of green on the trees, with snow still on the high hills and the midge, scourge of the Highlands, still relatively dormant. The moors and hills in late July to September, when the heather is in bloom and putting a reddish-purple gloss on the hillsides, are also beautiful, and so are the autumn colours of red and orange and saffron yellow in October when the bellows of the rutting stags are heard in the glens.

DO'S AND DON'TS

By and large, the relationship between landowner and walker/mountaineer in Scotland has been a good one, with most owners appreciating the walker's desire to walk and most walkers being sensitive about estate and farming needs, including calving and lambing times, grouse and deer stalking dates, respect for gates and fences, for young trees and growing crops. In a very real sense walkers have had a glorious freedom to walk but it carries responsibilities with it.

In general, the mere fact of being on wild land or proceeding across it is not, *by itself*, considered an offence but all land belongs to someone and the complex area of possible damage or intrusion can be involved.

Legal action means a breakdown in this informal relationship, but it is necessary to know what the law is as there are widespread misconceptions about it.

It is frequently said that there is no law of trespass in Scotland, but there is. It is different from the law of England and Wales.

In England, damages can be recovered from a trespasser almost as a matter of right through the civil courts. In Scotland, a landowner must prove that damage has been caused before being able successfully to sue the trespasser. It goes without saying that damage of any kind is thoroughly reprehensible and wrong.

Most landowners have no objections to walkers and mountaineers, and there is a cordial coexistence, but the law of Scotland makes it clear that a landowner is within his rights to ask a walker to leave his land and may, if necessary, use 'just sufficient force' to achieve that object. A landowner may go to court for an interdict to prevent trespass by a particular person but this would normally only be effective against a regular offender and would probably only apply to a highly sensitive local situation. An exception to this is the Trespass (Scotland) Act 1865, which means that the police *can* be involved if fires are lit without permission on private land or camping is carried out without permission.

Dogs: Where there are sheep around, dogs should be kept on a leash (they can be shot on sight if a shepherd has reasonable grounds for thinking sheep have been chased) and certainly under control at all times.

Gates: Gates must be shut after you unless they are already open when you get there, in which case they should be left open.

Fences: If you have to cross a fence, put your rucksack over first and do your utmost to cross without putting pressure on posts or wiring.

Litter: In addition to being ugly, plastic bags and other rubbish can maim or kill wild or farm animals which chew them. Take all rubbish home or place it in roadside bins. Broken glass can act as a magnifying lens for the sun's rays and start fires. Be extremely careful with matches and cigarette ends: ensure that they are totally extinguished and take them home with other rubbish.

Sheep: When sheep have lambs give them a wide berth in case you disturb ewes with sick young ones. If a lamb follows you, ignore it. If you see a shepherd and dogs driving sheep near you either get well out of the way or sit very still until they have passed you and are well clear. April and May are particularly sensitive times of the year.

Grouse: Grouse shooting starts on 12th August and has its peak during the rest of that month. It ends on 10th December.

Areas affected by it are normally clearly identified by the presence of shooting-butts, small palisades or 'bunkers' of stone and turf, wood or corrugated iron, which hold two or three people. Very few walks in this book are affected by grouse shooting and these are indicated. Stay well clear in season.

Red Deer: The season for shooting stags runs from 1st July–20th October and hinds from 21st October–15th February. In practice, the main time is *mid-August to around mid-October.* Few estates ask walkers to stay off the hills from July to February and those who do often put notices up to that effect, which are occasionally a bone of contention. Revenue from the letting of shooting rights or the commercial sale of venison is an important part of the finances of many estates. Hills like Ben Venue and Ben Ledi are not normally affected by deer stalking, but Ben Vorlich and Stuc a' Chroin at Loch Earn and their neighbouring hills and passes are; so are the Balquhidder Hills and some of the passes there. The golden rule in organising a hill-walking expedition during stalking dates is to check the position with the local estate. The police, Ranger-Naturalists, some tourism offices and main hotels can often supply addresses and phone numbers. It is traditional not to shoot on a Sunday (there are exceptions to this) but a Sunday expedition can move deer on, to the irritation of an estate plan for the Monday. Alternatively, if shooting is not taking place on a certain day most estates have no objection to walkers being on a particular hill that day. In some circumstances walkers on a hill can be of advantage to a shooting party in that they move the deer on to a desirable position. *There is no barrier to the use of Right of Way paths during the stalking or grouse seasons.*

WAY-MARKING

Many hundreds of acres of land referred to in this area are owned by the Forestry Commission and much has been done to deepen the interest and enjoyment of the tourist or visitor. The David Marshall Lodge, near Aberfoyle, is an attractive information and visitor centre and the area is dotted with picnic spots and secluded parking.

INTRODUCTION

The Commission have many way-marked (continuously signposted) paths in the forests offering walks of differing lengths. Some are scenically attractive while some are no more than forest 'roads' for taking timber out and marked with wayside poles with flashes of different colours to show the route. They cover a wide variety of scenery, however, and most give good rewards.

Way-marking, when it is taken on to hills and moors, is a controversial subject because of erosion problems and a loss of wilderness quality. Woodland walks can be done solely by following the markers but no one should start on a way-marked hill-walk such as Ben Ledi, Ben Venue or the Rowardennan shoulder of Ben Lomond without a map as objecting hill-walkers sometimes remove poles on higher ground.

When walking the way-marked Forestry Commission walks it is useful to have a note of the colour of the chevrons on the way-marker posts.

The colours for the following destinations are:

Aberfoyle (yellow); Kinlochard (blue);Trossachs (Brig o' Turk) (green); Callander (black); Gartmore (Cobleland) (orange); old Drymen/ Gartmore road (brown); Rowardennan (red); Inversnaid (white).

MAPS

This book has been written to be used in conjunction with the Ordnance Survey maps. The walks have been grouped together around Callander, Balquhidder, Aberfoyle and Loch Lomondside. Historic or scenic detail given in one walk will also apply to others, so it might be helpful to read all the walks in one section. With so many pass-routes some data is inevitably repeated.

The three sheets (1: 50,000) for the area covered by this book are: Stirling and the Trossachs, sheet 57; Loch Lomond, sheet 56; Loch Tay, sheet 51.

The Ordnance Survey also produce a useful Pathfinder series (1: 25,000) which gives much detail. The sheets needed for this book are: NN 20/30; NN 21/31; NS 29/39; NN 40/50; NN 41/51; NS 49/59.

There is also a tourist map available (one inch to the mile) entitled *Loch Lomond and the Trossachs.* Bartholomew produce a *Central Scotland* map (1: 100,000) which is useful for seeing the area at a glance.

The spelling of names poses a problem in that some are a corruption of the original Gaelic, and the meaning of some is a matter of debate. Ordnance Survey map spelling has been followed in most cases.

Walks mainly

linked to

Callander

Walk 1: The Wood Walk, 1 mile, half an hour plus, Callander. O.S. sheet 57.

Callander is a frontier town, one eye in the past cocked at friendly Stirling and the safer Lowlands where law and order occasionally ran, and the other on the Highlands where the clans gave endless headaches to what we would now call central government.

The Wood Walk is suitable for a short evening stroll, perhaps on the day of arrival, and is an appetiser for delights ahead. It gives a taste of the flavour.

Callander is not big—around 2,000 inhabitants or so—but it has long roots and a strategic position controlling key passes. It has heard the tramp of the Roman legions and the war-cries of the Caledonians.

Callander was written as Kalentare in 1504 and is thought to take its name from the name of a burn,

17

Caladar, which is probably close to the Gaelic form of the name. The early Celtic form is *caleto-dubron*, meaning hard water.

Half a mile to the west of the town, the River Teith, flowing through Loch Venachar, is joined by the River Leny from Loch Lubnaig.

It is said that the initial handful of houses were swelled by discharged soldiers from the Seven Years' War in 1763. The Crown Commissioners laid out its wide squares when the Drummond estates were forfeited after the 1745 Jacobite Rising. Further back the Livingstones—Earls of Callander—held sway. James VI entrusted his daughter, the Princess Elizabeth, later to become the Winter Queen of Bohemia, to their care and she was partly brought up in Callander.

It has ecclesiastical roots going back to long before the thirteenth century.

The Wood Walk was a favourite in the boom years when Sir Walter Scott's poem *The Lady of the Lake* caught public imagination and boosted tourism, which has stayed at a high level ever since. It is mandatory reading for a Trossachs holiday.

This walk, with its whispering trees, quiet glades and glimpses of hill and loch, is infectious.

Its attractions were also enjoyed by other literary figures, playwright J. M. Barrie (of *Peter Pan* fame) and A. J. Cronin, (*Hatter's Castle, Keys of the Kingdom*) and on whose writings BBC-TV based their popular series, 'Dr Finlay's Casebook', with Callander portrayed as Tannochbrae. You pass 'Arden House' on your way to the wood.

Novelist Annie S. Swan also knew Callander, living for a time at Milton, Loch Venacharside, and the

Wordsworths passed through on their Highland tours.

A longer walk, the Crags Walk, links with the Wood Walk but is treated separately.

Start at Bracklinn Road, which turns uphill from the Main Street, close to the post office at the Stirling (east) end of Callander. Proceed up Bracklinn Road (ignore the turning on the right) and go across the bridge which crosses the disused railway line, now fast disappearing under grass and housing development.

Large detached houses, built in Callander's hey-day as an up-market tourist resort, are on either side of the road.

Ignore Ancaster Road on the left, with the exception of looking over it where there is a fine view of Ben Ledi, dominating the town.

It is a beautiful mountain (2,875 feet). You can see its long south-east slope running down to Loch Venachar, which perhaps gave the mountain its name of *Beinn an Leothaid* (the mountain of the gentle slope), although another possibility is *Beinn le Dia*—mountain of God—a reference to sacred festivals in days long gone.

Ignore Avelard Road to the right and continue uphill until Bracklinn Road curves left, with a grass section on the immediate left. Watch out for 'Arden House', the building used in 'Dr Finlay's Casebook' as the home of Dr Cameron and Dr Finlay, and their pithy housekeeper, Janet. Bracklinn Road then swings uphill again (ignore the junction to the left).

A signpost at the corner says 'To Bracklinn Falls': follow that road uphill beside a wood and ignore a first, faint track that leads into the trees.

Another signpost is reached that says 'To The Crags, Bracklinn Falls and Red Well' (ignore) and 'To The Wood Walk' (take that).

A well-beaten track leads left through attractive woods of oak, birch, elm, plane, fir and pine.

The path is easily walked and has rest seats. At a well-made bridge a junction path branches off right to the top of the Callander Crags (ignore if only doing the Wood Walk). A seat in a gap gives an attractive glimpse of Loch Venachar (the pointed loch) and the Menteith Hills, and then the path goes quickly downhill to the Callander tennis courts. (Just before the finish of the Wood Walk the descent-path from the top of the Crags comes down and joins it.) From the tennis courts a side road leads back to the Main Street.

Walk 2: The Crags Walk, circular, 2 miles, Callander. O.S. sheet 57.

The Wood Walk is a stroll. The 1,000-foot Crags Walk (called Callander Craig on the map) is for the fit or those with time for plenty of rests. It is boggy here and there and stony and steep, so do not underestimate it.

The view from the top is magnificent, and shows clearly the green fields of the Lowlands gradually merging into moorland and the hills of the Trossachs. It is particularly attractive in the evening.

There are four permutations: (1) do the Wood Walk until you meet a junction path going (right) uphill to the top of the Crags, or (2) go up the steep track from the Callander tennis courts-end of the Wood Walk, which links with the upper track, or (3) drive up past the Bracklinn Falls road turn-off until you reach the crest of the metalled road which eventually goes near Braeleny Farm. Watch out for a sign (left) that says 'To Callander Crags'.

But the *best* way (4) is to drive to the Bracklinn Falls car park. Just *before* the park a Forestry Commission sign on the left says 'The Crags' and 'Upper Wood Walk'.

A *faint* path runs left. It is easy to miss. (A marker, on the other side of the road, is a bay with a seat.)

The path is mucky but easily followed: you pass some railings on the left. It crosses a ruined moss-covered drystane dyke and seems to go through the woods for a long way with no vistas. The path splits at a prominent oak: one trail goes steeply downhill to the tennis courts and ultimately the Main Street. The other goes *very* steeply uphill (right) to the Crags.

A break in the trees gives a welcome breather point with views to Loch Venachar, the Menteith Hills, and the roofs of Callander. Take a good look at the trees on the hillsides above Loch Venachar: a persistent story says they were originally laid out in the positions of the British Army at Quatre Bas, at the Battle of Waterloo (1815), but they have now been obscured.

The path continues steeply uphill. Beware of one sharp turn left where the path is slight: you immediately cross a stony section.

Panting, you reach a deer fence (with an older fence behind) and you are at the top. A Forestry Commission sign *on the fence* and *facing you* points right. If you decide to go left (south-west and then south) you descend steeply to Callander tennis courts (joining the end of the Wood Walk).

(Do not start muttering about the author if the left and rights get confused! The path is very steep and is immediately confronted at the top by the Commission's fence and sign. I am using left and right here *as one faces the sign*.)

Once on top, and turning round, and staring *over* the Crags at the view, the lefts and rights are, of course, reversed. (I have given the compass directions as well.)

To complete your circle back to the Bracklinn Falls car park follow the track east (right as you face the Commission's sign, left as you gain the top, turn round and stare out over Callander) along the lip of the Crags.

The views are exquisite.

You see to the east, the Braes of Doune and Uamh Mhór (see Walk 3, Bracklinn Falls), the far away Ochils (the ancient Celts called them *Uchil*—the high ground) and prominent Dumyat, the plain of the Forth with Grangemouth beyond, ahead the Touch Hills, Gargunnock, the Fintry and Campsie Hills, and the flat land around Menteith. To the south-west, Loch Venachar, and further round Ben Ledi: and the wooded Pass of Leny, of strategic importance in time of war.

Behind you is a great bowl of lonely moorland and hills. You can see Braeleny Farm, Beinn Each (mountain of the horses), Stuc a' Chroin (peak of the cloven hoof) and Ben Vorlich, and the ancient passes over to Loch Earnside and Glen Artney.

The deer fence ultimately changes direction and crosses your path, so to speak, and there is a stile.

You pass a small cairn commemorating Queen Victoria's diamond jubilee in 1897, erected by Malcolm Ferguson of Callander.

The path descends steeply to where a branch of the deer fence turns sharp left. The path becomes obscure and varied but if you stay with it you will reach the road at a point where there is a sign indicating the Crags for people going up that way.

Do not worry if you lose the path: make for the metalled road which can be seen, and then tramp downhill until you reach the Bracklinn Falls car park once more.

You pass a path on the right (worth a diversion) going to the Red Well (Chalybeate Spring), used in past centuries for medicinal purposes. It was restored by the Callander Amenity Committee in 1924, but became overgrown and has now been cleared again.

The Crags Walk was popular in Victorian times—they must have been hardy strollers.

Walk 3: Bracklinn Falls, half a mile, off the A.84 at Callander. O.S. sheet 57.

The name of these spectacular falls is spelled in various ways, Branklinn, Branklyn, Bracklinn, but there is little doubt about the derivation of the name.

Breac is the Gaelic for speckled (there is a Beinn Bhreac on the way up to Ben Venue). Alan Breck, in Robert Louis Stevenson's *Kidnapped*, was so named because he had a pock-marked face. *Linn* means a pool—the speckled pool, but the speckles are foam-flecked roaring water or, some argue, flood-carried debris.

The tourist in summer does not see the best of these falls because the water is low, but in early winter when there is much rain, or in spring when the snows are melting, the Keltie Water crashes through the narrow and steep rock walls—a fearsome sight.

It is a beautiful spot of lovely woods of oak, alder and birch lipping the gorge. Take care on the edges: a couple fell to their deaths in 1844. The name Kelty derives from *coilltidh* (a wooded place).

Follow the initial road route for the Wood Walk but drive or walk uphill (there is a signpost) until you see a sign, pointing right, indicating the car park.

A well-beaten track goes east, above the golf course, and through a wood. You pass two gates and well-sited seats, and get a good view of Dumyat Hill at Menstrie (Clackmannan) and Stirling Castle on its rock. Dumyat is so prominent you can see why the Picts placed a fort on its lower shoulder. The long line of the Campsie Hills, with Dumgoyne (another hill-fort) at the end, opens out to the right. They link (going left) with the Fintry Hills and the Gargunnock Hills.

Just before you descend to the falls you can see ahead the mound of Uamh Bheag and Uamh Mhór, the little and big caves, where Stevenson depicted Alan Breck and David Balfour lying out all night to escape the Redcoats.

Sir Walter Scott drew on the scene for his novel of the 1745 Rising, *Waverley*, and in front of friends rode a pony across the then flimsy bridge over the falls for a bet. The present structure is safe. It was rebuilt by the 2nd Troop, 11 Field Squadron, Royal Engineers in November 1976.

Scott, of course, brought the falls into *The Lady of the Lake*—the Highland hero Roderick Dhu was 'brave, but wild as Bracklin's thundering wave':

> As Bracklinn's chasm, so black and steep,
> Receives her roaring linn,
> As the dark caverns of the deep
> Suck the wild whirlpool in,
> So did the deep and darksome pass
> Devour the battle's mingled mass.

In the past, many people used to return to the main road by passing near Dalvey Farm and the ruins of Auchleshie, an old stronghold of the Clan Buchanan, and back into Callander by the road, but this way is now fenced off and the tarmac and traffic make it unpleasant.

It is probably best to use the falls as a browse-around place and then to return to the car park. When the water is low, families sometimes picnic in summer on the rocks upstream. Minor paths here are not recommended.

Connoisseurs of waterfalls should betake themselves further north up the A.84 to the narrow Pass of Leny, about a mile and a half from Callander.

As with Bracklinn, its most magnificent face shows itself outwith the tourist season.

Walk 4: Uamh Bheag (2,181 feet) and Uamh Mhór, 4½ miles north-east of Callander, there-and-back hill-walk of 9 miles in all. O.S. sheet 57.

When he was a boy, Robert Louis Stevenson spent holidays at Bridge of Allan, near Stirling, and the wide sweep of moorland culminating in Uamh Bheag, the little cave, is clearly seen from there.

The young Stevenson remembered this and brought the hill into his novel *Kidnapped*. He depicted Alan Breck Stewart and David Balfour sleeping on it during their fugitive flight south.

Sir Walter Scott also wrote of the hill and its shoulder, Uamh Mhór, the big cave, in the opening section of *The Lady of the Lake*. He had the stag from Glen Artney heading for there:

> With one brave bound the copse he clear'd,
> And, stretching forward free and far,
> Sought the wild heaths of Uam-Var.

Uamh Bheag (pronounced Ooav Vek) commands the best near view of these fine mountains, Stuc a' Chroin and Ben Vorlich.

The caves that give it its name are quite hard to find and are on its lower shoulder, Uamh Mhór. They can be found on the western shoulder at a prominent scarp of rock and close to a tiny 'canyon' or rift valley, known locally as 'Rob Roy's Cattle Fank' (pen).

Sir Walter wrote:

> Less loud the sounds of silvan war
> Disturb'd the heights of Uam-Var,
> And roused the cavern, where 't is told,
> A giant made his den of old.

Giants living in the caves are problematical but they were certainly a haven for 'broken men', fugitives on the losing side of power struggles.

As mentioned in the forthcoming Glen Artney section, the high-level fank is not far from the drovers' route up the Allt Ollach and over the *bealach* (pass) between Uamh Bheag and Beinn Odhar, and it was certainly known to the MacGregors.

Uamh Bheag is normally climbed from the Glen Artney side, or from near Doune, but for the purposes of this book I have outlined a way to and from the Bracklinn Falls.

Cross the falls bridge and go through the trees to the east side. At the left-hand corner is an iron gate. Immediately after that another gate takes you on to the hillside on the lower slopes of Tom Dubh (the black knoll). Walk over to a farm steading (building). Keep a wall to your left, Wester Bracklinn Farm down on your right and walk to another steading and gate. Please ensure to close all gates if they are closed when you get there. You pick up a broad track uphill which is slightly indistinct in places. Do *not* follow another track to the right.

You will strike a Land Rover track, shown on the map, which leads to the old ruined bothy of Leathan Dhail which, like its neighbour Arivurichardich across the way, was inhabited by a shepherd and family in living memory. This is a beautiful spot with good views to Ben Vorlich, Stuc a' Chroin and over the lower ground.

A modern bulldozed estate track has been constructed which runs north-east along the hill called Meall Leathan Dhail. If you follow the track it will take you to the east side of the hill where you drop down to the dip between it and the steep slopes of Uamh Bheag.

If you want to turn your back on the track and tramp over the crest-line of Meall Leathan Dhail you follow an old fence line.

The going is very rough with long heather and peat hags, and there are many boulders in the dip between the two hills. Watch out for an electrified fence, which can be easily crossed, with care, and without touching it.

You then toil to the top of Uamh Bheag. The all-round view is magnificent, the Menteith Hills, the Gargunnock Hills, the Campsies, Loch Venachar, the wooded top of Callander Crags, Ben Ledi, Beinn Each, and a splendid view into Gleann an Dubh Choirein. Ben Lawers is also seen and the Crianlarich Hills peep over. Ben Lomond and the Arrochar tops also show. Across the way, Stuc a' Chroin and Ben Vorlich show massive sides. There is a cairn and a fence junction on top. The trig point is on Uamh Mhór.

To return to the Bracklinn Falls, angle south-east down the Allt (burn) Ruith an Eas and when you near the trees above Wester Bracklinn Farm angle westwards until you pick up the way you came.

It is pleasant moorland walking with lovely pools and small waterfalls in the burn, hence the name *eas* (a waterfall).

This is really a walk for the fit but a family could manage it if there is an expert hill navigator present. The ground is rough and, in mist, often featureless. It is no place for the novice.

In spring, with the moorland birds arriving, the curlews and golden plovers, it can be magnificent.

Walk 5: Callander to Comrie, via Glen Artney, 13 miles, easy glen and pass hill-walk rising to 1,000 feet at the watershed. O.S. sheets 51 and 57.

This is an excellent trek to do soon after arriving in Callander because it was here that Scott set the opening scenes of *The Lady of the Lake.*

The hunters are pursuing a stag and drop out one by one until the boldest loses the stag and his horse but finds his Lady of the Lake.

The chase sweeps past Callander, up the valley of the Teith and into the Trossachs 'deepest nook'— twenty miles to the west:

> The stag at eve had drunk his fill,
> Where danced the moon on Monan's rill.
> And deep his midnight lair had made
> In lone Glenartney's hazel shade.

St Monan was a shadowy sixth-century saint, who was perhaps a companion of the great Brendan of Clonfert. His bones were taken to Scotland at the time of the Danish raids on Ireland and buried on the Fife coast. A veneration of him sprang up in different parts of Scotland. A rill is a burn.

There is a Rob Roy connection as well.

There are problems in trying to define the Rob Roy country as Rob's war travels took him to such diverse places as Kintail in the north-west, in the 1719 Jacobite Rising, and Sheriffmuir and Falkland, Fife, in the 1715 Rising, but Glen Artney has a more local claim.

He tried to capture a *spreidh* (herd) of cattle owned by Livingston of Bedlormie, in West Lothian, as it passed the Stirlingshire village of Kippen, but became involved in a skirmish with local people. Livingstone was anti-Jacobite. Rob Roy was so angered by this complication that he sent the *spreidh* north by Loch Ard and took cattle from every byre in Kippen to make a second herd and sent that down Glen Artney to be sold at Crieff.

This is a very attractive pass-crossing of high moors, fringing mountains and hills, chuckling burns and rivers, and rolling hill farmland.

It can be done in a return trip by using the bus but check locally as bus patterns in the Highlands can change radically from season to season.

From Comrie one can catch a bus to Crieff, change there, catch another to Stirling, change there, and catch another back to Callander. Otherwise, it is a car at each end and parties changing keys.

Sir Walter also brought the glen into his novel *The Legend of Montrose*, and he portrayed Sir Kenneth in *The Talisman* as coming from here.

The surrounding moors and hills are great havens for deer, both now and in past centuries.

It was a favourite hunting forest of the Scots kings and its hereditary Keepers were the Drummonds of Drummond Ernoch, near Comrie. The name is derived from Earn, really Eireannach, from Ireland. One of them was involved in a grisly sixteenth-century incident with the MacGregors, which is told under the section dealing with the Loch Earn pass, Walk 9.

In 1622 when James VI of Scotland was in London, as James I of England after the Union of the Crowns in 1603, he heard there was a white hind in the Corrie Ba area of the Blackmount Hills, near Bridge of Orchy, and not far from the modern road to Glen Coe.

He sent one John Scandoner, from Windsor, accompanied by two attendants, to try and capture it with the help of the local clansmen and aided by Sir Duncan Campbell of Glenorchy, the famous Black Duncan of the Cowl or the Seven Castles.

The bid failed so they were sent to Glen Artney, then owned by the Earl of Perth, to capture roe- and red deer alive and send them to London and also to get practice for a further bid on the white hind.

It is one of the most southern deer forests and its distinguished guests have included the Prince Consort, Albert, who shot his first stag there as a guest of the Drummonds.

Take the metalled road up past the Bracklinn Falls and follow it to the farm at Braeleny. You pass through two gates, one below the farm and the other beyond the farm buildings.

The road beyond the farm deteriorates into a stony track. There are fine views ahead to Stuc a' Chroin (peak of the cloven hoof) with the old bothy of Arivurichardich at its foot. The bothy stands near part of the route to Stuc a' Chroin and another hill-pass to south Loch Earn via the south-eastern shoulder of Ben Vorlich, and is dealt with in a separate section, Walk 10.

To your right are the heather slopes of Uamh Mhór and Uamh Bheag.

You pass a modern water-point 'house' on your right and then reach a well-constructed wooden bridge across a ford where the Keltie Water swings north-east and is absorbed into the Callander reservoir.

The route from here over the pass to near Glenartney Lodge is a signposted Right of Way which means you can walk it any time in the stalking or grouse shooting season but you must stick to the path (the old track is indistinct, to say the least, in the early section) at these dates. Restrictions off the path still apply.

Just after leaving the Right of Way sign, go uphill to a gate and you will find a well-made modern track with attractive scenery all round. There are good, backward, views to the lonely corners up Gleann a' Chroin and the Bealach nan Cabar (pass of the antler: a favourite crossing for deer) into Glen Ample.

As you cross the watershed, many grouse will probably fly up, cackling 'go-back, go-back', but walk on and enjoy the views back to Ben Ledi and the wide sweep of moorland. You drop down to a steep gorge and cross the Allt an Dubh Choirein (the burn of the black corrie) by a bridge, and then reach a gate and deer fence. There are fine views down the long length of Glen Artney. A corrie, incidentally, is from the Gaelic *coire*, a bowl-like hollow in the hills. It also means kettle (but not our modern kind), a bowl or cauldron.

You pass Glenartney Lodge where Rudyard Kipling and his wife once recuperated after his illness.

Next, you go through two gates and reach the road close to Auchinner near the wide waters of the Water of Ruchill. The Right of Way ends here.

The terrain widens and becomes more fertile and the lower reaches of the glen are beautifully wooded.

You have three options at this point: (1) to proceed down the metalled road on the south bank of the Water of Ruchill to Comrie, or (2) to proceed down the road as far as Dalchruin, take the left fork and cross the Water of Ruchill by a bridge near

Dalclathick, or (3) to go left at the road-end near Auchinner and proceed down the north bank of the river.

My own preference is for route two because it avoids complications at Auchinner if there are farm animals around. It does mean some hard-surface tramping though.

Keep an eye out on the right for the little church of Glen Artney which has Drummond heraldic decoration but is fairly modern.

You pass, too, on all three routes the famous Spùt a' Chleibh, the Spout of Dalness, where the water can foam white and where salmon can be seen jumping in season.

When you are at the Glenartney Lodge and Auchinner road-end look out on the right for the Allt Ollach which leads to a *bealach* (pass). This was the route used by the cattle drovers heading for the Falkirk fair. It was their last big climb before they descended by the Garvald Burn to the Braes of Doune and the low ground from then on.

They reached the head of Glen Artney by coming directly across the hills from St Fillans, probably by the Strath a' Ghlinne and Gleann Ghòinean.

When Crieff was the market the drovers crossed from Loch Tayside, via Glen Lednock, to Comrie.

If you want to take route one you leave the track at the Glen Artney estate road (left). The Right of Way has ended. On the other side is a building, 'Staghorn'. You go left past that along the road to a track going (right) past Auchinner. Continue on to a bridge over the Allt Strath a' Ghlinne just before it reaches the Water of Ruchill. Cross and go east on a track high above the river. It peters out after about half a mile and you reach a Land Rover track which swings north at Dalclathick. Here a little used track runs parallel to the river. You pass through deep woods and the remains of old townships which show how well populated this glen was in past centuries. At Dalrannoch Farm a narrow road runs down to the A.85 and thence to Comrie.

If taking route two at the lodge road-end you pass through a gate on to the metalled main glen road south of the river. Remember that when you swing left at Dalchruin to cross the river, you then pass over two bridges in succession. Faint paths run parallel to the Water of Ruchill. Take the lower path at junctions. These are beautiful woods of hazel, birch and pine. Complete into Comrie as route one.

Comrie is worth a lengthy visit and has a beautiful site in the strath of Upper Strathearn, an extension of fertile Strathmore.

It has several links with Callander. It, too, lies on or near the geological feature of the Highland Boundary Fault and has more recorded earthquake tremors than anywhere else in Britain. In 1839 the entire district shuddered and people fainted or ran out into the streets.

The name Comrie derives from *comhruith*, the confluence of streams—the Earn, the Lednock and the Water of Ruchill.

Like Callander, it was a frontier town in past centuries between Lowland Scots and Gaelic-speaking Highlanders.

Roman camps and a fort at Comrie had links with the fort at Bochastle at Callander.

The ruins of old townships can be seen in many glens.

You pass Dalginross on your way into Comrie, on the plain of Ruchill.

The monument on Dunmore Hill is to Henry Dundas, Viscount Melville (1742–1811), one of the most powerful men in Scotland and First Lord of the Admiralty and Secretary for War in Pitt's administration during the Napoleonic Wars.

At the junction of the Glen Artney road and the B.827 you pass the Territorial Army camp at Cultybraggan which held German prisoners during part of the Second World War.

The Ross 'suburb' of Comrie was a seventeenth-century tartan-weaving clachan and the Scottish Tartans Museum in the town is well worth a visit.

The Campbells, a branch of the Lawers line, had lands here too. Sir Colin Campbell of Aberuchill and Kilbryde was Lord Justice Clerk in the seventeenth century and one of those who paid blackmail to Rob Roy.

And that is, almost, where we came in.

Walk 6: Ben Ledi (2,875 feet), 4 miles plus, hill-walk, 2 miles from Callander, A.84 and A.821, four permutations. O.S. sheet 57.

If you want to see treasures of silver and green then take yourself off to Ben Ledi, familiar in shape to every TV viewer who watched 'Dr Finlay's Casebook'. It was the hill that figured in the opening shots of Tannochbrae with the river and swans in the foreground.

The green is the hill and woods and the silver is the area's lochs. Ben Ledi is a fine place to view many of them.

As mentioned in Walk 1, the Wood Walk, the name of Ben Ledi may derive from *Beinn an Leothaid*, the mountain of the gentle slope. That is the south-east section that runs down to the long Loch Venachar.

Another suggestion is *Beinn le Dia*, the mountain of God or of light. The connection is with *La Buidhe* (pronounced Boo-ee) *Bealltuinn* (Beltane), the Yellow Day of the Fires of Bel.

In past centuries, on the first day of May, the old Celtic New Year, young folk from the parishes of Callander, Buchanan, Balquhidder and Aberfoyle met on the summit of Ben Ledi to commemorate an old Druidic rite—the lighting of the Bealltuinn fires. Bel (from *Be'uill*, Life of All) had been the early Celtic sun god.

In former days all the hearth fires in the Highlands and Islands were extinguished before midnight to symbolise the dying of the old year. New sacrificial fires were kindled on local hill-tops and the hearth fires relit from the purifying hill-top flames. The ceremonies included a feast and several rites, such as driving cattle between two fires of Bel to free them of disease in the coming year. These rites were later reduced to a bonfire, a token leap through the flames, and shared food.

On top of the hill, on smooth turf, a bannock was prepared from oatmeal, eggs and milk. A fire was lit and when it died down the bannock was cooked on a stone set in the ashes. It was then cut into slices, one of which was marked with charcoal. The slices were put into a bonnet and handed round the company. It was said that whoever drew the marked portion had to skip three times through the embers.

Ben Ledi is thought to have been chosen because of its conspicuous site, wide views, and central accessibility.

From Ben Ledi's top one can see to the south-west, Loch Achray (the loch of the level field) near the Trossachs Hotel: nearer at hand, Loch Lubnaig (loch of the little bend) bounds its north-eastern side: Loch Katrine lies to the west and there are glimpses of Loch Doine and Loch Voil, (*a' bheothail*, of the quick-running flood) in Balquhidder of the Braes.

To the south is the Lake of Menteith and tucked away in the woods are Loch Drunkie and Loch Rusky.

Nearby—and bewildering to those using old maps—is the Glen Finglas reservoir, above Brig o' Turk (bridge of the boar).

Ben Ledi dominates the passes north and south and to the west, and it is not surprising that the probing Roman armies built a temporary fort at Bochastle, near the crossroads at Kilmahog.

This fort had links with another at the Lake of Menteith and the camps and fort at Comrie.

Scott wrote in *The Lady of the Lake*:

> On Bochastle the mouldering lines,
> Where Rome, the Empress of the world,
> of yore her eagle wings unfurl'd.

Almost opposite, on Dunmore Hill, on Ben Ledi's eastern slopes, the Caledonians built their much older fort and both sets of fighting men must have warily eyed the other's movements.

There are four main ways up the Ben.

The first is to drive from Callander to the crossroads at Kilmahog, and turn left on to the A.821. Kilmahog is thought to have been named after the cell (*kil*) of the Celtic saint, St Chug. However, another theory concerning the name is that it derives from Cocca, a reputed robemaker and cook to St Patrick and St Columba.

In past times Kilmahog also housed a community of millers.

Look out for a huge boulder perched on the hillside (to the right), known locally as Samson's Putting Stone. It is said to have been hurled there in a difference of opinion between two Celtic giants; others prefer the version that it was deposited by a glacier.

Some years ago the most popular way up Ben Ledi was from the farmhouse at Coilantogle where the long, gradual, grassy, south-east shoulder ran to the top of the Ben.

Scott's *The Lady of the Lake* helped popularise this, but it can cause problems for the farmer, and in recent years the most used route has switched to the Loch Lubnaig side.

The farm was described in *The Lady of the Lake* as Clan Alpin's (another name for the MacGregors) outmost guard and Sir Walter made Loch Venachar the scene of the duel between Roderick Dhu and Fitz-James:

> Till past Clan-Alpine's outmost guard,
> as far as Coilantogle's ford.

And also:

> Here Vennachar in silver flows,
> There, ridge on ridge, Benledi rose.

39

There is no ford now. It disappeared when the old Glasgow Corporation built sluices to control the outflow to the Teith and compensate for the loss of water from the Loch Katrine reservoir.

In Scott's poem, the Fiery Cross which was carried by runners to raise the MacGregors for war does not got as far east as Kilmahog.

He routes young Angus as striking north round the base of Ben Ledi, between the mountain and the River Leny, where the Callander-Oban railway and the eighteenth-century military road used to run.

Further along from Coilantogle is the farmhouse of Milton, which used to have a herd of shaggy West Highland cattle which Landseer used in his paintings. It was also the home for a time of the writer Annie S. Swan.

To climb Ben Ledi on the Loch Lubnaig side drive on the A.84 (T) to the bridge across the Leny at the start of Loch Lubnaig. Just across the bridge one can park beside the disused railway line which now leads to the Forestry Commission's holiday cottages further up the loch.

Cross a marked stile on the west side of the road and go up a very eroded path through the trees. This way has become so eroded and mucky in recent years that the walker should really think twice about using it. There are now duckboards in some sections.

Once clear of the trees you find a fence and another stile which takes you quickly to a burn which you cross and then proceed up the hillside, parallel to the cliffs on the east side, until you are obviously clear of all problems and can gain the ridge which runs from Coilantogle to the top of the Ben. This hillside has had marker poles which have been removed from time to time, but the way is clear enough.

If returning the same way, ensure you are far enough down the south-east ridge to be clear of all bluffs before you drop down, turn north, and return the way you came to the car park.

Another popular way in the past, walking in from near Kilmahog over Bochastle Hill, has been ploughed up for forestry and is also very boggy. But it is to the north and north-east that the Ben has its most spectacular side.

To the east is the narrow Pass of Leny with its steep sides and roaring river, making it easy in past centuries for the clans to block or defend it, and hard for the road, rail and bridge builders of modern times to find a route.

Edward Caulfield, General Wade's subordinate, built the military road into Strathyre on the west bank of the river, and a century later the railway engineers took the same line. The railway fell a victim to Dr Beeching's cuts. The present-day A.84 road takes the east bank and one can catch glimpses of both the old military road and disused railway across the river.

It was here that Sir Walter Scott portrayed the Earl of Menteith and his servants meeting Dugald Dalgetty in his novel *The Legend of Montrose*. Also on this side, but with the Leny and Loch Lubnaig between the Ben and the main road, is St Bride's chapel, the ancient burial place of the Mackinlays who had lands here and one of whose name became the twenty-fourth President of the United States of America. The chapel is covered in a separate section, Walk 8.

Sir Walter wrote of the summoning of the clans:

CALLANDER

Benledi saw the Cross of Fire,
It glanced like lightning up Strath-Ire.

Where the Fiery Cross once sped its urgent message there are now the ruins of old townships, and where the black cattle once grazed there are now modern farms, flocks of sheep and acres of trees.

The fourth most attractive (and most difficult) way up the Ben is to cross the bridge near the start of Loch Lubnaig and then walk up the track past cottages at Coireachrombie and parallel to the disused railway line.

On this side of the mountain is the Stank Glen, an ugly name for a glen of great beauty. The name is a corruption of a Gaelic word *stang* (pools).

After passing Coireachrombie you *pass* a forestry road going left. Near the glen proper you pass through a Forestry Commission boom-gate and the forestry road takes a sharp curve.

The old path used to go up through the trees from here but at the time of writing is 'lost'. It was buried in the mammoth storm of 1968 and since then forestry roads have been made. The forestry road sweeps round and back like a hairpin and you can either walk round and back on it or push your way through the trees to meet it again as it comes back towards the glen. The path goes up through the trees from the road's (top) side with the burn on your right. This section of forest seems to get worked on a lot. The path is hard to spot. If in doubt, push up the Stank Glen keeping the gorge and burn on your right.

It becomes easier later. Watch out for a fine waterfall on the right further up the glen. The path takes the walker clear of the trees into the back corrie of Ben Ledi, a place of wildness, of red deer in the area outside the deer fences, of huge boulders and pinnacles on the north side of the Ben.

When the trees end you can proceed to the head of the corrie and gain the ridge at the lowest point and then follow it to the top. This route has been way-marked in recent years but the poles vanish on the upper ground.

Those accustomed to rough scrambling and hill-walking can turn sharp left immediately after the trees end on the left, go uphill, cross a deer fence by a stile and can rest at some boulders as big as cottages. They contain some short practice rock climbs and provide rough shelter for people sleeping overnight.

A tiny burn runs down the steep hill to the left (as one looks up) of the large pinnacles and a faint track on its bank takes the walker high up on the Ben, where he can gain the ridge and then follow the fence to the summit trig point.

The way up the Stank Glen and straight over the dip near Creag na h-Iolaire (rock of the eagle, pronounced Crek na Uoo-lar) used to be an ancient pass. A small lochan lies there, known as Lochan nan Corp, the small loch of the bodies.

A funeral party walking from Gleann Casaig to St Bride's chapel tried to cross this lochan when it was frozen. The ice broke, and many were drowned.

On top of Ben Ledi there are magnificent views to the Menteith Hills and the lower ground, to nearby Stuc a' Chroin and Ben Vorlich at Loch Earn, and to the lonely country between Ben Ledi and Balquhidder.

There are also good views northwards towards Ardnandave (or Armandave) Hill at the bend in Loch

Lubnaig which the Wordsworths admired when they toured the Trossachs.

A recommended round trip is to ascend by the Stank Glen and partially descend by the south-east ridge and then north, down through the trees, to the Leny Bridge car park.

A fine high-level expedition for those mountain-fit and well practised is to ascend Ben Ledi and then cross to Balquhidder, via the northern ridge, Creag na h-Iolaire, detour to Ardnandave Hill, back to Stuc Dhubh, on to Benvane and down its long northern shoulder to Ballimore where you can be picked up again by car.

Walk 7: Ben Gullipen (1,380 feet) and Beinn Dearg (1,420 feet). O.S. sheet 57.

The small, heather-covered hills of Ben Gullipen (the mountain of the curlew) and Beinn Dearg (the red mountain), between Loch Venachar and the A.81, draw the eye as one nears Callander from the south or south-east.

Care is needed in ascending because the hillsides are used as farm grazing.

From the A.81, about half a mile south of Kilmahog, a gate takes the walker on to the north-east slopes of Cock Hill and thence on to Ben Gullipen. The hill has two moundy tops with the north-west one being the higher.

It and the neighbouring Beinn Dearg cradle the lovely, secluded Loch Balloch (from *bealach*, a pass). Crossing the dip between the two tops is an easy stroll. There are problems in descending from Beinn Dearg because of trees and it is best simply to make Ben Gullipen a single hill-walk and go back the way you came. This is suitable for an afternoon or evening stroll.

There are lovely fringe-of-the-Highlands views, including little Loch Rusky across the road.

Walk 8: Pass of Leny, short strolls from the Falls of Leny car park, A.84 (T), in pleasant woodland, plus high-level viewpoints for the spry. O.S. sheet 57.

About a mile north of Kilmahog the River Leny takes a sharp twist east and thunders through a narrow gorge.

It is a favourite spot for visitors but in summer the water, although fast and white, can be low compared with the fearsome roaring floods of spring and winter.

The name was written as Lani in 1237 and Lanyn in 1238 and is derived from the Gaelic *lanaigh* (boggy meadow or marsh).

The narrows of the pass were of strategic importance long ago, and between here and present-day Callander there was a 'spat' in 1645 during the Scottish Wars of the Covenant when a punitive force of Campbells, out to harry the lands of clans supporting the cause of Charles I, were ambushed and routed.

The woodland and plant-life is very rich.

Across the road from the falls—take care in crossing in summer as traffic is heavy—is a car park constructed by Stirling District Council.

Like the small park built near Inverlochlarig, Balquhidder, it is an excellent one of its kind—thoughtfully made and, in this case, well-screened by trees. There is a path-indicator board.

There is a walk-path to the falls constructed on Farmston estate ground.

Three way-marked walks start at the back of the car park and of these the third is by far the best. The first is an easy stroll.

If going to the top of Meall Garbh (the rounded rough hill) remember that the ascent and descents are steep and stony.

In summer, when the ground can be dry and dusty, the descent from the highest point can be almost too rough for shoes or casual footwear.

The first walk, Option 'A', runs for about quarter of a mile and follows an old charcoal burner packhorse track to a viewpoint. You can see the flat round platforms where charcoal was made from tree branches. You walk back the same way to your starting point.

Option 'B' (one even gets bureaucracy in the outdoors) is three-quarters of a mile, and lasts about an hour but you can obviously make your own time. It climbs to the top of beautiful oak woods and into pine, spruce and larch woods and has a separate way down.

The third, 'C', is about a mile and takes you to the highest points where you can do a full circuit back to the car park, the whole route being about one and a half miles and lasting one and a half hours or longer if you, rightly, want to savour the views.

The first viewpoint gives a bird's eye look southwards down the Pass of Leny to Callander with the Ochil Hills seen sideways-on beyond that and the prominent hill of Dumyat (pronounced Dum-eye-at) at its western end. It is a good place to appreciate the roughness of the Highlands fading into the smoothness of the Lowlands.

As you go higher you appreciate these lovely woods and can look across to Ben Ledi.

At a junction there is a notice, 'Meall Garbh walk' (go left).

As you go higher you come to a knoll, with a rusty fence and quartz veins forming an almost perfect triangle on a rock. It is worth pausing here to look to Ben Ledi across the way and to Ardnandave Hill which Dorothy Wordsworth noted when she was driving south with her brother on 10th September 1803. The Fergusons had one of their leading houses at its foot. The name derives from *Ardandamh* (height of the stag).

You also look down on St Bride's chapel between the River Leny and the road, the Mackinlay country and the south end of Glen Ample.

The little secluded graveyard attracted much attention in 1982, the 150th anniversary of Sir Walter Scott's death.

In the early nineteenth century people literally queued to look at it and in the twentieth century thousands of tourist cars and coaches drive past, many unaware that it is a site of some significance.

Inside the walls of the graveyard can be seen the faint outlines of St Bride's chapel, a name that dates back to Celtic Church times, and despite the roar of passing traffic a few feet away it can be a surprisingly attractive spot with the River Leny rippling past on the other side and large pine trees whispering overhead.

Sir Walter, in *The Lady of the Lake*, portrayed young Angus arriving breathless with the Fiery Cross at the chapel just as a wedding was taking place. (He erroneously called the river the Teith.) Nothing must halt Clan Alpin going to war and Sir Walter depicts Norman of Armandave saying farewell to his weeping bride and instantly heading for the rallying ground.

A tablet by the gateway says the foundations were identified and restored in 1932 to commemorate the centenary of the death of Sir Walter, 'whose romantic genius still lays enchantment on the countryside'. Underneath are the words *Bheir sibh Urram do m'ionaid naomh* (Ye shall reverence my sanctuary).

Also near the top of the hill, to the left of the path, is a prominent rock with views to the Menteith Hills, Beinn Dearg and Ben Gullipen.

The top is flat and tree fringed with a wide outlook to Ben Ledi, the Menteith Hills, the Gargunnock and Fintry Hills, the Ochils, Stirling Castle and the tower of the Wallace Monument.

It is a similar view to that from Callander Crags (which can be seen) but much wider.

Uamh Mhór and Uamh Bheag show up to the east and so does the prominent Creag an Eireannaich in the Balquhidder Hills.

Remember, the descent-path can be steep and stony. Take care.

Go quietly in these lovely woods. On one visit recently I saw jays, roe-deer, a buzzard, and many woodland birds.

Walk 9: The Loch Earn Pass (Bealach Dearg), a magnificent 12-mile glen and hill-pass cross-route from Ardvorlich, south Loch Earn road, to Callander (15 miles if you have to walk in from the A.84 (T) road junction along the south Loch Earn road to Ardvorlich). O.S. sheets 51 and 57.

Logically, this route should start from Callander like the others in this section but it is probably best done from the Loch Earn side.

The Bealach Dearg (*bealach* is the Gaelic for pass and *dearg,* pronounced jerrak, means red) is packed with historical interest and crosses the eastern shoulders of these two fine Munro mountains, Ben Vorlich and Stuc a' Chroin.

A Munro is an individual mountain over 3,000 feet, first catalogued by Sir Hugh T. Munro, president of the Scottish Mountaineering Club from 1894 to 1897. The Munro lists are revised from time to time in the light of modern map-making and there are currently 278 of them in Scotland. Munro-bagging is a pursuit followed by a growing number of hill-walkers.

This walk, of course, does not go to the summits but passes over their shoulders at a height of around 1,970 feet.

It is a pass-crossing of great antiquity and much used in past centuries.

Sir Walter—who else—knew the area well, and in *The Lady of the Lake* he wrote:

> But, when the sun his beacon red
> Had kindled on Benvoirlich's head,
> The deep-mouthed bloodhound's heavy bay
> Resounded up the rocky way,
> And faint from farther distance borne,
> Were heard the clanging hoof and horn.

You need a helpful friend to drop you off at the south Loch Earn road or hitch up the A.84 until about half a mile from Lochearnhead where you will see the south Loch Earn road junction.

Go east for about three miles to the *east* gate of Ardvorlich estate. Keep an eye out for Edinample Castle on your left near the entrance to Glen Ample. It was held by the Breadalbane Campbells as part of their sixteenth- and seventeenth-century expansionist policies.

Loch Earn is said to derive its name from the Irish influence of the early Christian era but erne is also another name for the sea eagle which formerly nested on inland lochs as well as on sea cliffs. The bird became extinct but attempts are being made to reintroduce it from Norway on to the western seaboard of Scotland.

You pass some cottages and the west entrance to Ardvorlich House. The east entrance is just past a hump bridge.

It is worth pausing at Ardvorlich, which has been held by the Stewarts for centuries. A stone marks the spot where seven Macdonalds of Glen Coe were buried after being killed when raiding Ardvorlich in 1620.

Scott, in his novel *The Legend of Montrose*, called it Darlinvarach Castle.

The name, Ardvorlich, is said to derive from *Ard Mhurlaig* (or *Mur-Bhalg*), promontory of the sea-bay, and as Loch Earn is a freshwater loch this is a puzzle. The name was apparently sometimes used when an inland loch looked like a sea loch. There is another Munro hill called Ben Vorlich at Loch Lomond and it, too, could be said to have the same kind of outlook.

At Ardvorlich is a family talisman called the *Clach Dhearg* (the red stone), which is secured with silver hoops and fitted with a chain, and is said to have miraculous properties. If the stone is dipped in a pail of water and moved thrice, sunwise, round the pail, the water would then have healing powers in illnesses relating to cattle. Old accounts tell of people resorting to the stone for cattle disease. There is a tradition that it dates from the fourteenth century and was brought back from the Crusades. (Walter Scott portayed Sir Kenneth, Glen Artney and the Crusades in his novel *The Talisman*.)

The house also contains the Glenbuckie Stone which should be dipped in water by the lady of the house or a guest who can then drink and utter a wish.

In addition, the house was the scene of a horrific sixteenth-century incident.

Stewart of Ardvorlich had married the daughter of Drummond of Drummond Ernoch, the king's Keeper of the royal forest of Glen Artney and Steward of Strathearn.

Drummond cut the ears off some MacGregors whom he had found poaching but their friends later took their revenge. They captured him, cut his head off and took it to his daughter's home at Ardvorlich.

Keeping the head hidden they asked for food and, in the manner of Highland hospitality, she put bread, cheese and oatcakes on the table and left the room. When she returned, her father's head was on the table with bread and cheese stuffed into his mouth.

The daughter, who was then pregnant, was so shocked that she fled to the mountain shielings and gave birth there to a son. A lochan, un-named on modern maps, is called the Woman's Loch (Lochan na Mnà).

The baby, James, grew into a moody youth and later became one of the Marquis of Montrose's staff officers. He murdered Lord Kilpont in a brawl in Montrose's camp during the 1645 campaign of the Scottish Wars of the Covenant.

To go over the pass, or to climb Ben Vorlich from this side, take the broad track with farm buildings starting to appear ahead. At a junction go right (as if you were going to the 'big house') across a bridge, then sharp left and uphill, passing through a gate. You are now following the west bank of the beautiful main glen burn.

You will see an estate notice saying the route to Ben Vorlich is marked by poles and requesting that you stick to the path. (See separate section, Walk 10, for the ascent of Ben Vorlich.)

Once on the way uphill *do not* go through a small gate to your left—it leads into a private section of woodland.

Look out for the ruins of an old mill on your left.

You proceed upwards beside attractive woodland, cross a second gate (stile), and, if you pause for a breather, you have a good view back to Loch Earn and Ardvorlich House.

The woods become more attractive and Ben Vorlich starts to show up ahead.

You pass through a deer fence (stile) but *do not* detour left to a bridge across the burn which can be seen from this point.

Stay on the track and pass through another gate (stile).

Just past a small bridge of sleepers across a small burn a grassy side track goes off left as the main track swings away from the burn. Take this left track (as you face up). At this point the steep east sides of Ben Vorlich start to dominate.

The ground becomes marshy, but stick to the burn and the path reappears. Look out for the remains of old shielings.

As the trees end, make for the notch between Ben Vorlich and Meall na Fearna.

A tributary burn has to be crossed, and the ground gets wilder and rougher as one gets up into the corrie. The ground becomes boggy, and there are more ruins of shielings.

Keep going until you reach the narrow pass between Ben Vorlich and Meall na Fearna. This is a very attractive and wild section. Look out for a couple of home-made howffs (shelters) made by hill-walkers for sleeping overnight in the narrows of the pass.

You pass an old fence and wall and then descend (south) over rough ground down the glen (Ben Vorlich's south-east shoulder on your right) to the ruins of the old shepherd's cottage at Dubh Choirein (the black corrie) where two burns join to form the Allt an Dubh Choirein.

It is worth while spending some time there savouring what it must have been like living in such a remote spot, cradled by hills, and with supplies brought by pony from Glen Artney or over the pass from Callander.

At this point you might feel daunted because you now have to pull up to the dip between Meall na h-Iolaire and the long south-east shoulder of Stuc a' Chroin.

Meall na h-Iolaire is pronounced Mee-owl na Yoo-lar and means the rounded hill of the eagles. Examine the hillside closely, because tracked vehicles have scored the ground and these look like paths. The dip is ahead and slightly to the right.

Before describing how to find the best track up, it must be said that many hill-walkers ford the burn here. But downstream to your left, out of sight, is a bridge beside a waterfall and pool. There is a snag in reaching it in that you have to cross the tributary burn of the glen you came down to get to it. Once across the bridge, turn right and follow the Allt an Dubh Choirein until you are almost opposite the ruins. Then set off uphill.

Watch out for a faint path, with a firm gravel base in the early sections, wending its way across the moor. It will take you high up before it vanishes in boggy ground. If you fail to find it, make your own way up to the lowest point. The slopes up to the dip are gradual and easily ascended.

At the head of the pass you come across large peat banks.

The easiest way down to the bothy at Arivurichardich is sometimes hard to find. The Callander reservoir and Gleann a' Chroin lie below you. Between you and the foot of the glen you will see a fence and a gate. Most people head for that and angle down to the bothy.

However, above the fence, a path can be picked up which runs parallel to the fence and then cuts down. This makes for easy walking at a pleasant angle along the hillside but there are a couple of sheep tracks in the same corner which peter out. If you are fortunate enough to strike this path, fine. If not, make your own way down, muttering.

The bothy was lived in by a shepherd and family within living memory but is now locked and used by the local estate for sheep-rearing purposes.

The site is an old one and the long name intrigues many. Seton Gordon, that peerless Scottish naturalist, historian and mountaineer, said it derived from Airigh Mhuircheartaich. *Airigh* is the Gaelic for a shieling and the rest is a man's name. Moriarty is a derivation of it.

From there, tramp southwards down the track, passing the entrance to Glen Artney, cross the Kelty Water by the bridge and continue down to Braeleny Farm.

A car can be brought from Callander to just short of the farm, thus saving some weary miles on tarmac back to the town.

Two cautionary words: the map shows a continuous path all the way. In fact, it vanishes from time to time. Do not walk it in the grouse shooting season or at stalking times.

It is a walk of great contrasts, wooded glen, high corries, hill-passes and tracks, and gives excellent rewards.

Walk 10: Ben Vorlich (3,224 feet), 4 miles south-east from Lochearnhead. Stuc a' Chroin (3,189 feet), 1¼ miles south-west from Ben Vorlich. O.S. sheets 51 and 57.

These attractive hills are clearly seen to the right of the blue wall of the Grampians when viewed from Stirling, with the prominent notch which gives Stuc a' Chroin its name (peak of the cloven hoof) showing up well.

From Callander they are rather retiring. Coming down Glen Ogle from the north they present a bold front. Ben Vorlich (mountain of the sea-bay) has an attractive cone-like shape when viewed from the Perth road or the Glen Artney side.

In winter, care is needed because they both have steep sides and Stuc a' Chroin has cliffs and rough rock. In summer they make for very pleasant high-level walking.

They dominate the high ground between Loch Earn and Glen Artney, and are among the most attractive hills in this book.

This chapter should be read in conjunction with Walk 5, Callander–Comrie and Walk 9, Ardvorlich–Callander (Bealach Dearg).

Ben Vorlich is most frequently ascended from Ardvorlich. You take the route from the east entrance at Ardvorlich as described for the Bealach Dearg crossing to Callander, but after about a mile leave the glen and go up the rounded north ridge.

The estate has put in marker-poles but these sometimes disappear.

The upper part is steep and broad and you reach the top ridge *west* of the summit. You will find an old fence. Follow that almost due *east* to the top. There are two tops, close together, with a very slight dip in between. The more easterly is the summit and has a cairn, and there are attractive mountain views all round.

Ben Vorlich is a favourite place for people to spend the night out or to watch the sun coming up. If you do decide to do that remember that it is a bare mountain with little shelter. A small hollow, just down from the top and facing Stuc a' Chroin, can take three people and their sleeping bags in comfort but not much more.

To get on to Stuc a' Chroin follow a broken fence down to the Bealach an Dubh Choirein by way of the steep south-west spur. The buttress of the mountain rises straight ahead but can be walked up by keeping slightly to the right (north-west). It needs some care and some minor scrambling. From Stuc a' Chroin you then face a descent into Glen Ample and a walk back to Ardvorlich or Lochearnhead along the south Loch Earn road which, however, is not recommended.

Stuc a' Chroin is often climbed from the Callander side, from Arivurlchardlch. The pleasant, slanting path to the Meall na h-Iolaire *bealach* (pass) is very hard to find, but it can be picked up just beyond the highest of the fences behind the bothy. Otherwise go along Gleann a' Chroin, past the reservoir, and follow a prominent burn northwards uphill to the pass. You then have to climb up on to the eastern shoulder, followed by an easy walk along the long ridge.

The walk ends at the final scree and stone-covered climb to the top. The summit is flattish and has two cairns.

This is probably the safest way to the top of Stuc a' Chroin as it avoids any bluffs.

This route is sometimes combined with an ascent of Ben Vorlich by descending Stuc a' Chroin's steep sides (where care is needed) to the Bealach an Dubh Choirein, the linking ridge, walking over to Ben Vorlich and then descending from the summit down Ben Vorlich's south-east shoulder to Gleann an Dubh Choirein. You then return to Arivurichardich by the route described in the Ardvorlich–Callander (Bealach Dearg) walk. This can be a long day, with a climb up to the pass at the end of it, but it can be a very worthwhile one, nevertheless.

In recent years estate notices have been erected in Glen Ample, which flanks these hills to the west, stating that there is no access to these hills from there.

Some experienced hill-walkers ignore these and continue to ascend from that glen in a time-honoured fashion. They park at Ardchullarie at the south end of Glen Ample, climb steeply up on to the ridge at Beinn Each, the peak of the horses, follow the ridge (along which a fence runs) over Stuc a' Chroin to Ben Vorlich, descend down to Glen Ample and walk back up the glen to Ardchullarie. A similar prohibition currently applies at the Loch Earn end of Glen Ample where some hill-walkers go up Glen Ample to beyond Glen Ample House, follow a bulldozed 'road' up the hillside round Creagan nan Gabhar and into a fine corrie, and thence ascend Ben Vorlich by its north-west ridge. From there, a popular route runs on to Stuc a' Chroin, descending, with care, down Stuc a' Chroin's steep north-west ridge back into the glen. The remains of old shielings are to be seen on the shoulder of Creag Dhubh.

This route is a very pleasant one. (Glen Ample is a Right of Way and is treated separately.)

The writer's preference is to do each hill singly (purely a subjective view). Ben Vorlich from Ardvorlich and Stuc a' Chroin from Arivurichardich. They are both worth spending time on.

The best walk for the hill-fit, or for strugglers who plan to make a day of it, is probably to make the round trip from Arivurichardich to Stuc a' Chroin, on to Ben Vorlich, descend to Gleann an Dubh Choirein, climb up and over to Arivurichardich and down to Braeleny (or, if you have no car, on to Callander). It is about fourteen miles but, if you have no car and are walking from Callander, it is over twenty miles.

As with other walks in this section please take note of the deer and grouse shooting dates.

Walk 11: Glen Ample (Loch Lubnaig to Loch Earn, or vice versa), 7½ miles, 3 hours, Right of Way glen walk. O.S. sheets 51 and 57.

This glen is an ancient crossing route and was once part of a hunting forest of the Scottish kings, which stretched as far as Glen Artney.

Despite the numbers walking this Right of Way pass, deer can often be seen on the hills on either side and, in winter, in the glen itself.

The name Ample means vessel-shaped (ampoule is from the same derivation), that is, bowl-shaped but elongated and narrow at each end. It is best to walk it from Ardchullarie More, on the Loch Lubnaig side (A.84) and to finish at Edinample, Loch Earn.

There is parking space for a few cars at the Ardchullarie end and the track is well-decorated with estate notices.

The white mansion-house of Ardchullarie was once the home of the Abyssinian traveller Bruce of Kinnaird, who retired and died there. His discoveries of the source of the Blue Nile and other finds were ridiculed at the time. He wrote five volumes there about his Abyssinian travels, published towards the end of the eighteenth century.

The name Ardchullarie (pronounced Ardwho-olaree) probably means the high recess of the King, a reference to the royal hunting forest.

The old house features in Scott's novel, *The Legend of Montrose.* It was from here that the Earl of Menteith rode east with Dugald Dalgetty to meet the Highland chiefs assembled at the castle of Darlinvarach (Ardvorlich) at Loch Earn.

The way goes steeply up through pleasant woods, and once the crest of the pass is reached it eases off into a broad track and runs down the length of the glen. It is muddy in places. Near the house of Glenample you cross small burns. If they are running high there is a bridge on the higher ground near the house on one of the subsidiary burns on the east side of the glen, and one close to the house itself which crosses the Ample Burn.

There are fine mountains on the east flank, Beinn Each, the outliers of Stuc a' Chroin, Ben Vorlich, plus a high hill pass used by deer, Bealach nan Cabar, which goes over to the head of Gleann a' Chroin and the wonderfully named bothy of Arivurichardich.

You pass the remains of old shielings in this once empty glen and a glance at the map and the remnants of the Gaelic names shows that the people once knew every corrie and knoll—you can see Baile a' Mhaoir (the wood of the bailiff's township), Meall nan Uamh (round hill of the caves), Ben Our (*Odhar*, dun-coloured mountain), Creagan nan Gabhar (rock of the goats), Allt a' Choire Fhuadaraich (*fuadrach*, the hurrying burn of the corrie), Creag a' Mhadaidh (rock of the fox), Meall nan Oighreag (round-shaped hill of the cloudberry) and many others.

The path wends alongside the Ample Burn and attractive alder-fringed pools and ends at the Edinample Bridge on the narrow south Loch Earn road.

Watch out at this end for some fine falls and an incredibly perched Scots pine—the MacGregor emblem—overhanging the river and with its roots clinging tenaciously to the rocks.

Go west along the road a little and you will get a good view of the mainly sixteenth-century (it has earlier roots) castle of Edinample, once a MacGregor stronghold and later taken over by the encroaching Campbells.

The name Edinample is from the Gaelic *aodann* (face), i.e. hill-face.

In 1982 the northern section of the glen was planted with conifer trees on the west side, greatly changing its face and reducing both the number of deer and their winter sheltering areas.

This side was also a favourite deer calving place in June but this area, too, has been vastly reduced.

Walk 12: Western hills, Glen Ample, 9 miles, hill-walk for the nimble and the spry starting at the Edinample end and returning by the glen. O.S. sheets 51 and 57.

To get another view of the attractions of Glen Ample it is worth going up on the lower hills on the west of the glen, traversing the crests and then dropping down to Glen Ample and returning by the glen path to Edinample.

Access here has been greatly changed by the 1982 forestry planting (see Walk 11, Glen Ample), but it is still possible to gain the hill crest by making your way up the hillside, outside the new fence, to the summit of Meall nan Uamh (round hill of the caves) and then on to Meall nan Oighreag (round-shaped hill of the cloudberry) and along the crests to Sgiath a' Chàise.

As you ascend you get good views of Beinn Each and across to Stuc a' Chroin. Ben Vorlich shows its cone face.

There are excellent views to Loch Voil and Loch Doine at Balquhidder and to the big hills of Stob Binnein and Ben More.

The Ben Lawers group and their neighbour of Meall nan Tarmachan are also clearly seen.

It is pleasant to sit and look across the glen at the 'big corrie' hills. The line of Glen Ogle is seen to the north, the main route to the west and also north to Glen Coe and Fort William. A military road ran along there in the eighteenth century and part of it can be seen from the present-day road.

If conditions are good you can also see from these hills an interesting ecological development. A straight line of trees bisects the west side of Glen Ogle. This marks the old line of the railway which was 'lifted' in 1965 (a landslide hastened its end a month before the scheduled removal date of October).

When the railway was in being most young trees attempting to grow at the side of the tracks were cut down and sheep were kept out. Now the track has gone, the boundary fences are still reasonably intact and the sheep could not readily harm new growing trees. Consequently, a line of large birches runs unmolested along the hillside, evidence of what much of Scotland must have looked like before that devouring monster, the sheep, stripped the hills. The track line is now an attractive way-marked walk from Lochearnhead. Queen Victoria thought Glen Ogle was like Afghanistan and, indeed, the name is said to derive from Gaelic words for dread or forbidding.

Ben Lomond and Benvane (Balquhidder) show up to the south-west and further along Beinn an t-Sithein at Strathyre and Ben Ledi, near Callander, also come into view. It is best not to continue along to Creag a' Mhadaidh (pronounced Crek a Vatee, rock of the fox) as the hillsides to the glen become rough and steep.

Drop down east from a dip where good smooth turf changes into tussocks and then turn (left, north) down a 'shelf' until you descend down steep slopes to the Glen Ample burn. Return down the glen to Edinample.

Walks mainly

linked to

Balquhidder

Walk 13: Creag an Tuirc, circular, 1 mile, Balquhidder church, Kirkton of Balquhidder, off the A.84. O.S. sheets 51 and 57.

A very popular Scottish folk-song is now entitled 'The Wild Mountain Thyme' or 'Lassie Will Ye Go' but its real name is 'The Braes of Balquhidder', and it was written by the Paisley-born weaver-poet Robert Tannahill (1774–1810).

To see the lovely braes and a magnificent view, go to the top of the Manse Rock, or Creag an Tuirc (rock of the boar), which overlooks the village and its renowed church site which goes back many centuries.

You are in a historic setting. The lands of Balquhidder parish were in crown ownership as far back as the time of James IV and formed part of the dowry given to the Welsh princess, Margaret Tudor.

It was a glen of the clans, MacGregors, Fergusons, Stewarts and MacLarens. Creag an Tuirc marked the gathering place of the Clan MacLaren who retain the rock in their care to this day. They were a courageous lot and, even after the Jacobite Rising of 1745 had failed, they still truculently continued to bear arms and wear white cockades.

They and the MacGregors had a fight in 1532 over who had the right to be seated first in the church.

Rob Roy MacGregor, famed cattle-dealer and warrior, is buried in the old kirkyard, as is his wife Mary (Helen), and sons Coll and Robert.

The 'modern' church (1855) is bracketed by a path on either side: both join up and ascend through the woods beside Kirkton Glen.

If you initially take the burn path a notice points right and says 'Footpath'. Take this path to the right.

Follow a wide track uphill through pleasant woods of fir and larch. Look back before you start and you will see to the east the cone-shaped peak of Ben Vorlich at Loch Earn.

You pass a sign on your left, with an arrow on its far side, pointing right. Ignore it. It was rather loose when I was last there and may have been removed by now. It marks the path you return on.

You soon see a Forestry Commission sign which says 'Straight On To Kirkton Glen, Right Creag an Tuirc'. You pass an old sheep tank (pen) almost smothered in trees.

Watch out for a small sign on the right of the path (it is easily missed) which marks where you leave it. If you hate signs, look for a break in the trees and a crumbling drystane dyke with a gap in it.

You then come on to the top of the crag amid some fine pines. There is a log seat.

The view takes the breath away. The fifteen-mile length of the glen stretches out, both Loch Voil and Loch Doine (the names mean muddy and quick-running respectively) catching the eye. In clear weather, the house of Inverlochlarig at the head of the glen, where Rob Roy died in 1734, can be seen. The striking peak of Stob a' Choin (point of the dog) is on the left at the head of the glen and Benvane and Glen Buckie are across the way. The houses, fields and river stretch out below, and to the left Ben Vorlich and Stuc a' Chroin lift proud heads, with the tip of Beinn Each also peeping over.

The large mansion-house of Stronvar (formerly a youth hostel) can be seen across the glen. It is now a guest house.

The opening shots of the film *Geordie*, the story of a small boy who grew up to be an Olympic hammer-thrower, were filmed from this rock.

Robert Louis Stevenson brought Balquhidder into *Kidnapped* and also the sequel *Catriona*. Sir Walter Scott, a lawyer, first visited the district to serve a writ of evictment on a MacLaren of Invernenty in 1790 and talked with elderly men who had fought for Bonnie Prince Charlie. He heard tales of Rob Roy, stayed to marvel, and subsequently wrote his famous novel *Rob Roy.* The glen was, of course, also a MacGregor stronghold.

Another literary figure, William Wordsworth, wrote his poem 'The Solitary Reaper' after watching the Balquhidder girls singing Gaelic songs as they brought in the harvest.

This is one of the area's best viewpoints.

Faint tracks run east and can take you clear of the trees and on to the open hillside of Auchtoomore, beside an ancient fank, but that way is not recommended: there is an attractive view of Ben Vorlich and Stuc a' Chroin, but you still have to pick a precarious way down through the lower woods to the road, although you can get clear if you go far enough along.

On the crag a Forestry Commission notice says 'Forest Walk'. Go back that way to complete the loop. It is way-marked (posts with yellow tops) but be careful if the ground is wet. The track is steep and greasy and faint in places. If in doubt, go back down the way you came.

The way-marked track takes you back to the one you came up (watch out for an unexpected sharp turn to the right before the paths join), and you return to the church.

Treasure this view: many a MacLaren heading for battle must have left it with reluctance.

Walk 14: The Kirkton Pass, Balquhidder to Glen Dochart, 6½ miles, glen and hill-walk. O.S. sheet 51.

Before the days of helicopter gunships, radar and night-sights, a soldier, as Alan Breck says in Stevenson's *Kidnapped*, could check no more ground than that covered by his boot soles.

The MacGregors, MacLarens and others were superlative hillmen and could outwit most pursuers.

The hills were rougher then than they are now, the heather was longer and more wild and cover was more plentiful. The old phrase for a fugitive was to say he was 'in the heather'.

Balquhidder has several 'escape' glens or passes and they provide excellent walking.

BALQUHIDDER

A favourite walk in recent years was from the old youth hostel at Monachyle, up the Monachyle glen and over to Glen Dochart by the Garbh Bhealach, the rough pass. Unfortunately, the Glen Dochart side is now affected by tree planting.

Rob Roy and his wife Mary lived for a time at Monachyle Tuarach (across the loch from Monachyle) before going to Inverlochlarig Beag around 1722. He also had a house at Auchinchisallen (also described as Auchinchallan) in Glen Dochart, given to him by the Earl of Breadalbane, and later burned by Swiss mercenaries following his Jacobite activities and outlawing.

Rob Roy also knew the Kirkton Pass and this gives a flavour to such walks.

Again, it is a route that needs a car at each end. Those going from the Balquhidder end have the best of the bargain.

Before going over the pass it is worth having a good look at the Kirkton church and graveyard. The Kirkton church is beside the road from the valley of the River Balvag to Loch Voil and the mouth of Glen Buckie, and was a natural meeting-place.

The present-day church was built in 1855. The ruined church, dated 1631, is built on top of a pre-Reformation church which itself dates back to the thirteenth century or earlier. It was known as the *Eaglais Bheag* or Little Church.

The walls can be seen near Rob Roy's grave.

A monastic cell, the Oratory of St Angus—the patron saint of Balquhidder—stood in a field below the church.

A church bell dating from 1684 sits on top of a chest and an older one is inside. The St Angus Stone (on the north wall) dates from around A.D. 750–850 and the font from around A.D. 1200–1400. There are other historical and religious memorabilia as well.

The parish is associated with the MacLarens, the Fergusons, the MacGregors and the Stewarts of Glen Buckie.

The Reverend Robert Kirk, Gaelic scholar, student of faery lore, and author of *The Secret Commonwealth of Elves, Fauns and Fairies* (see Walk 21, Doon Hill, Aberfoyle), ministered here from 1664–1685. His wife is buried here.

Rob Roy and his family are, of course, buried here as well. It is worth noting that the bell which is inside the chest was once pinched by Rob Roy and presented to a school! It took a couple of centuries to get it back.

The church and the surrounding area have been the scene of clashes of a decidedly irreligious nature.

Nearby the annual fair of St Angus was held on the flats between Glen Buckie and Auchtoo.

It was once the scene of a bloody fight after one of the Buchanans of Leny, at St Kessog's fair, Callander, accidentally knocked off a MacLaren's bonnet with a salmon that he was carrying. He was challenged to repeat it at the next St Angus fair, but the Buchanans attended in force. The quarrelling spread into a brawl, and the brawl into a pitched battle. The MacLarens attacked in a disorganised fashion, were beaten back, rallied, and eventually drove the Buchanans back down the Balvag amid great carnage.

The church, too, was the scene of a macabre oath-taking in 1589. The MacGregors, who had cut the head off the king's Keeper in Glen Artney (see Walk 9, Ardvorlich–Callander (Bealach Dearg)), took it to the church, placed it on the altar, and swore on their dirks that all would take the blame and all would defend the guilty. At that time they were proscribed, one of a series of dreadful acts of persecution by royalty or powerful enemies, ranging from their very name being banned, mothers being branded, children being taken away, weapons forbidden, baptism refused, and bounties on their heads. Mastiffs were kept to hunt them. The name *chon*, dog or hound (as in Loch Chon, Stob a' Choin), generally means places where deer hounds or mastiffs were kept.

A track (no gate) runs to the right of the church grounds and at the top there is a stile and a sign which says 'Kirkton Glen Walks'.

The track leads up through pleasant woods until another sign is reached. One way goes right to 'Creag an Tuirc', the other goes on up Kirkton Glen.

Further up the glen there is a junction of forest tracks, with a signpost saying 'Forest Walk'. You reach another junction with a broad track going right. Posts and a chain lie across the track ahead: step over or around them and continue up the glen. You pass another junction, but keep straight ahead.

As you near the end of the woods you have good views of the bold rocky face of Creag an Eireannaich, the Rock of the Irishman, a link with the Celtic Church missionaries. Another theory says it is Leum nan Eireannach, the Irishman's Leap. It is not named on the map but the small loch at its foot is.

You reach yet another junction with posts and a chain. On the left is a 'Forest Walk' but your way lies straight ahead and is signposted 'Glen Dochart path'. If the sign has vanished by the time you read this, it is the smallish path straight ahead going up through the trees (ignore the track going right).

When you emerge from the trees you see Creag an Eireannaich ahead, but do not head straight for it. Ignore a brightly coloured and striped pole to your right. A well-beaten path lips the woods at first on the left and goes up to the crags in zig-zags, taking the easiest ground.

The crag itself is a favourite place for members of the Ochils Mountaineering Club who produced a guide to the rock climbs on it and its surrounding boulders, some of which are very large.

You pass huge boulders on your right, and soon reach the lovely lochan, its banks occasionally marred by litter. The view back down the glen is attractive.

This track used to be way-marked but the markers have gone: no matter, the path is easily followed to the crest of the pass.

To descend to Glen Dochart, pass through a fence and gate close to the lochan and just after that the path goes down steeply to moorland, with good views to Ben More and Stob Binnein and to the Glen Lochay Hills.

(When coming from the north, and once over the pass, the way down into the Kirkton glen woods can be puzzling. Look for the line of the burn and stay roughly 'central' and you will pick up the zig-zags of the path. A tall pole, with the remnants of red paint on it, stands near the wood and marks the path. Look in this centre section for two fence posts of wood, close together, and with a metal one supported by an angled side strut: the path goes beside them.)

When leaving the head of the pass to descend to Glen Dochart, the path becomes faint with no way-markers, which is a blessing, because this is a beautifully attractive, wild setting.

Stob Binnein and Ben More are prominent on the left as you descend and Glen Dochart and the hill of Sgiath Chùil (the back wing) show up well.

Down on the left are the ruins of old shielings. Angle down to the Ledcharrie Burn and you will pick up the path again and some markers which lead to a prominent knoll with a marker on it used, alas, as a dump for litter by people too lazy to take it home.

The path runs down beside the burn, passes through a gap in a fence, goes under the bridge of the now disused railway line, crosses a 'field' and under a pylon line until it reaches the farm of Ledcharrie.

Pass through the yard (gate), keeping the house on your right.

(For those starting from Ledcharrie there is a parking place a hundred yards or so along to the west.)

Walk 15: Balquhidder (Ballimore) to Brig o' Turk, 8 miles, hill-pass. O.S. sheet 57.

'Come ye from Balwhither? The name of it makes all there is of me rejoice', says Catriona as she greets David Balfour in Robert Louis Stevenson's sequel to *Kidnapped*.

Balwhither is, of course, Balquhidder (pronounced Balwhidder), and although nowadays the name is applied to the whole of the lovely fifteen-mile glen, the name itself means the township in the back-country.

Balquhidder pulsates to historical memories and this walk takes us from it by another old hill-pass to Brig o' Turk (*Drochaid an Tuirc*, Bridge of the Boar) on the busy A.821 close to Loch Venachar and Loch Achray.

It is a walk of two halves—the first beautiful and almost wild and the second marred by modern, although no doubt necessary, development. Try it in late summer when the heather is out and splashing the hillsides with purple.

The first section after the head of the pass is in Gleann nam Meann, from the Gaelic *meann* (young roes).

About six miles from Ballimore, where Glen Finglas comes in to join Gleann nam Meann from the north-west, was an ancient burial ground attributed to St Kessog. Nearby Gleann Casaig is a variation of the name.

Both glens were part of a royal deer forest and the Stuart kings from James II onwards came here to hunt.

When James VI of Scotland went south to London in 1603 (the Union of the Crowns) as James I of England, poaching increased. In 1611 it was reported that the men of Glen Gyle, Loch Katrineside, Balquhidder and Strathyre had killed some deer and the Privy Council of 1612 outlawed the leaders.

In the early nineteenth century ponies with smuggled whisky passed up and down this pass.

In past centuries both glens were held by the Stewarts, along with some MacGregors.

BALQUHIDDER

Drive north up the A.84, past Strathyre, and turn left into Balquhidder Glen at Kingshouse Hotel, once the site of a military barracks and mail and coach halt, hence King's House, i.e. the king's representatives.

Just past the church a secondary road goes left, crosses the River Balvag at the mouth of Loch Voil and goes up historic Glen Buckie to the farm at Ballimore.

Your car driver will have to go home, but a service bus (from the Trossachs pier) passes Brig o' Turk and will take you back into Callander. Check the times locally.

It is a walk best undertaken from Balquhidder to Brig o' Turk and *not* the reverse.

In past centuries it was one of the ways used by the clansmen and women who lived in Balquhidder —the MacLarens, the Stewarts, the Fergusons, and MacGregors—to reach Menteith or Aberfoyle.

Savour it well: reivers, packmen, hunters, royalty and 'broken men' (the remnants of lost causes) have all trodden its tracks.

The going is boggy here and there but nowhere difficult.

A stone bridge crosses the Calair Burn beside Ballimore Farm. Cross a cattle-grid at the gate to Immeroin Farm, and look out for a sign (right) which says 'Footpath to Brig o' Turk via Glen Finglas, 8 miles'.

The path follows the south side of the burn and passes through a gate in a drystane dyke. A dyke in Scotland is a stone wall. The path occasionally vanishes or divides, but with the burn to your right and the north slopes of the nose of the long shoulder of Benvane to your left it is easily picked up again.

BALQUHIDDER

An old Land Rover track can be seen on the far side of the burn, but most of the time is not too obvious and there are lovely views back to Glen Buckie.

Just before the path rounds the nose of Bealach a' Chonnaidh and goes sharply southwards look out for the ruins of shielings.

These were the temporary spring and summer dwellings of the Gaelic people when whole families left their glen homes and headed for the fine hill grazing with their cattle and goats in an attractive pastoral pattern. There was joy at the end of winter. Cheese and butter were made and cattle fattened. Some of the loveliest Gaelic songs and poetry were written at or about the shieling life.

This corner of the route, which opens out into a green bowl in the hills, is very beautiful. A heather knoll beside the path gives a good view of a modern pastoral scene, with a foot-bridge, pens, hut and wide grazing for many sheep, at a point where the Allt Fathan Glinne joins the main Calair Burn.

As the path makes the long, but easy, climb to the *bealach* (pass) a fence can be seen on the right. There are boggy patches, but take time to look back at this lovely glen. Across the intervening hills, to the north, the sawn-off flat top of 3,827-foot Stob Binnein draws the eye.

A fence and gate mark the head of the pass.

A large cairn, which on close examination looks like an obsolete grouse-butt with some stones on top, lies just over the crest.

In the distance the Campsie Hills lie straight ahead, with the prominent stub of Dumgoyne clearly seen at the right end.

The waters of the Glen Finglas reservoir (the Lower Clyde Waterworks) glint at the foot of the glen.

The path continues downhill, but is swamped by a modern bulldozed Land Rover track. You can follow the intermittent path, walk on the Land Rover track, or follow the burn, the Allt Gleann nam Meann.

The Land Rover track follows the east side of the reservoir, with the eastern slopes of Benvane on your left. The old Glen Finglas, much of it now under water, opens out to the right.

This was a once beautiful glen, attractively wooded. An ancient legend tells of two travellers accosted by two beautiful maidens. One was lured away but the other closed his eyes and prayed. The one who had been lured away was found dead next day with his throat torn out. There is surely a moral there somewhere.

(If doing the route in reverse a signpost directs the walker off the Land Rover track on to the hill-path.)

A fence and gate are passed, and then, alas, tarmac takes over beside the reservoir, and after that it is just steady thud-tramping until one reaches the houses at Brig o' Turk. Ben Ledi comes into view on the left.

The glen below the dam is beautifully wooded, with much juniper on the lower slopes—it is said that in 1500, when the plague threatened, the glen's inhabitants burned juniper three times a day to keep the disease away.

Watch out for several charming cottages and, beside the school, an ancient graveyard where Stewarts and MacGregors are buried.

Glen Finglas has many literary associations. Scott's first verse composition was the ballad of 'Glenfinlas', written in 1799 under the influence of James MacPherson's Ossianic 'translations'. Scott visited the glen and the poem tells of a fatal hunting expedition sub-titled 'Lord Ronald's Coronach'.

BALQUHIDDER

The poem spurred James Hogg, the Ettrick Shepherd, to visit the glen. Scott brought it into *The Lady of the Lake* in the early stanzas about the chase of the stag from Glen Artney when Fitz-James found himself far ahead of his companions:

Few were the stragglers, following far,
That reach'd the lake of Vennachar;
And when the Brigg of Turk was won,
The headmost horseman rode alone.

There was once a wooden foot-bridge and causeway. The present bridge dates from the beginning of the nineteenth century.

The name *Finglas* means fair and green. The grass takes on a bleached appearance in winter.

It used to be a favourite haunt for artists and distinguished visitors, including Queen Victoria in 1869.

In the summer of 1853 it was the scene of a romance that startled fashionable society.

John Ruskin was on holiday here with his wife, Euphemia Gray, and his friend John Everett Millais. The painter's brother, William, and Ruskin's friend, Sir Henry Acland, the physician, were also in the party.

Millais painted a portrait of Ruskin, but he also fell in love with Euphemia. The Ruskins' marriage was later annulled and Millais and Euphemia were married.

There are two other interesting sites close to Brig o' Turk. A side road leads to 'Duncraggan huts' and it was here that Scott, in *The Lady of the Lake*, depicted Malise, the bearer of the Fiery Cross, bursting in on the mourners lamenting the death of Duncan and handing the Cross over to his son, Angus, the new chieftain.

Lendrick House, to the east, is now a youth hostel and was once a hunting lodge of the Earls of Moray.

Walk 16: Benvane (2,685 feet), Glen Buckie, Balquhidder, 4¼ miles, hill-walk. O.S. sheet 57.

People differ on the meaning of the name of this fine hill: most Balquhidder people say that the name derives from the Gaelic word *bàn* (white) because its north-facing slopes hold snow far into the spring.

Others say it is from *meadhon* (pronounced mee-un), the middle mountain. Certainly, it has a central position, although retiring, and it therefore has views far more striking than many a higher hill and is greatly underrated.

The answer is probably that both names are correct—it depended on where one lived in past centuries. Hill-walkers in Ireland today, where the glens are still inhabited, will find that some hills have two names and the choice of which will depend on your viewing location. The Irish Ordnance Survey maps give both names in such cases.

This corner between Balquhidder and Strathyre is very beautiful and was of importance in the past as a 'trade route'. Glen Buckie runs from Balquhidder along the east side of Benvane and its lower flats are attractively wooded and were well-populated in days of yore.

The upper glen is wide and sunny, and dotted with the ruins of shielings, firm evidence of a past population.

BALQUHIDDER

It used to be a royal hunting forest, and the Stuart kings frequently travelled from Stirling to hunt there or resided at nearby Ardchullarie (see Walk 11, Glen Ample).

A pleasant round trip is to drive to Balquhidder village and take the left road fork just at the east end of Loch Voil.

The metalled road narrows—take care on corners —and runs past attractive cottages and parallel to the Calair Burn almost due south until it ends at the farm of Ballimore (the big township), one of two farms (Immeroin is the other) which are all that is left of many ancient townships.

At Ballimore there is room to park at the roadside. Cross the bridge over the burn and ascend due south over Benvane's long north-west shoulder marked Lianach on the map. You pass the sign indicating the route to Brig o' Turk and go steeply uphill.

Look out for a hollow in some rocks once you gain the shoulder; it is a good shelter. (One of the theories of the meaning of the name Lianach is that it includes an old Gaelic word for stone.)

The view from the top is magnificent, with the Crianlarich mountains, the nearby Trossachs hills, and the Arrochar Hills, all clearly seen, plus fine views to Balquhidder, to Gleann nam Meann and down Loch Lubnaig. It is like Beinn an t-Sithein, Strathyre, only better.

The linking ridge to Ben Ledi is attractive.

Various return permutations are open—back down the way you came or contour north-west into Gleann nam Meann at the head of the pass and then follow the track round Bealach a' Chonnaidh and back to Ballimore, or descend into Glen Buckie.

If descending into Glen Buckie take great care to pick a safe way down clear of the crags. It is easy, provided one can see and one is nimble on steep slopes.

If in doubt, go back down the ridge until one is clear of Creag a' Mhadaidh (pronounced Crek a Vatee, rock of the fox), and then descend into the upper section of the glen.

At the time of writing forestry trenching is appearing so scrutinise your descent line well.

Tramp down to the track leading from the Ballimore road-end to Immeroin, and return to the road.

As with many glens and passes, you are following in the steps of many figures from the past, although most went over to Brig o' Turk.

The glen folk would be accustomed to seeing drovers and pedlars, packmen and pony trains carrying illicit whisky in the days when more strict excise laws were applied to Scotland after the Act of Union.

The lower glen, near the road, was once the site of iron smelting, and as this route was toll-free very large numbers of cattle, particularly in the eighteenth and nineteenth centuries, were driven via this glen to the big fairs at Falkirk. Old reports speak of many trees, and of meadows and cornfields. There is a tradition of a hospice for plague victims.

Glen Buckie was a Stewart glen and Stewart of Glenbuckie led the Balquhidder Stewarts in the 1745 Jacobite Rising, and was found shot in a mysterious incident in Leny House, a Buchanan holding.

After the '45, Colin Campbell of Glenure, the so-called Red Fox, administered the forfeited Appin

Stewart estates on behalf of the Hanoverian government. It was David Stewart, brother of the Laird of Glen Buckie, who warned Alan Breck in France of the danger of arrest in connection with the Appin murder. Robert Louis Stevenson brought this murder into his novel *Kidnapped*, when the Red Fox, on his way to evict Stewart tenants, was shot in the presence of David Balfour. It is based on a true incident, of course, and the Appin murder is one of the most intriguing of unsolved Scottish mysteries. An innocent man, James Stewart of the Glens, was hanged for it and a monument to him can be seen at the road bridge at Ballachulish, near where he was executed.

Dr Archie Cameron, brother of Cameron of Lochiel, the last Jacobite to be hanged, was said to have been captured by the Redcoats in Glen Buckie, but a stronger tradition would appear to place the arrest on Loch Katrineside (see Walk 32, Ben A'n). D. K. Broster, in her popular novel of the post-'45 period, *The Gleam in the North* (the sequel to *The Flight of the Heron*), sets the arrest in Glen Buckie.

Walk 17: Stob a' Choin (2,839 feet), 3½ miles. 2 miles south-west of Inverlochlarig, Balquhidder. Hill-walk for the fit and experienced. O.S. sheets 56 and 57.

The steep-sided Stob a' Choin (the dog's point) has great character and gives something of the true flavour of the wild country between Balquhidder and Loch Katrine.

It tends to be under-visited, and yet it has more attractions than, say, Beinn Tulaichean (the knolly hill), one of a cluster of Munro-tops on the other side of the glen.

In past centuries its name was a land title—Baron Stob-Chon—one of the feudal baronies abolished by the government in 1748 as part of the crack-down on the Jacobite lairds and chiefs. Rob Roy's youngest son, Robin, shot John MacLaren, Baron Stob-Chon, when he was ploughing and was outlawed for this act in a complex feud.

It is a hill with splendid views, and from it one can appreciate the northern passes or escape routes from Balquhidder over to Glen Dochart by Kirkton Glen, Monachyle Glen or Inverlochlarig Glen, to the south by Invernenty Burn, Glen Sgionie or the Allt a' Choin, or to the west by the Bealach nan Corp, or to Glen Falloch.

The fugitive King Robert the Bruce also hid in this area after the disastrous Battle of Methven, and there is a Bruce Cave at King's Rock, Craigruie, midway up Loch Voil on the north side.

Drive up the length of Balquhidder Glen to near Inverlochlarig until you see, on the left, a small car park and shelter erected by Stirling District Council, a well-designed and 'natural' pull-in point, more sensitively erected than many others elsewhere in Scotland.

You are very much in the Rob Roy country here. He died at Inverlochlarig Beag in 1734 and various place-names recall other prominent MacGregors or Stewarts.

Alexander Stewart of Invernahyle—who was related to the MacLarens—was 'out' in the 1715 and

1745 Jacobite Risings, and fought a friendly duel with Rob Roy. After Baron Stob-Chon's murder he reported Rob Roy's son to the authorities.

Two alehouses were formerly operated at Inverlochlarig by MacGregors who had prudently changed their names.

The house of Monachyle Tuarach, on the south side of Loch Doine, was in Rob Roy's hands when he was twenty-one, and the MacGregors were also involved with the MacLaren townships of Easter and Wester Invernenty (now since vanished), in the glen below Stob a' Choin.

Donald MacLaren, of Easter Invernenty, led the clan in the '45 and was wounded at Culloden. He had his home burned but daringly escaped when en route to Carlisle as a prisoner (an incident used by Sir Walter Scott in *Redgauntlet*), and thereafter lived happily in Balquhidder disguised as a woman until the Amnesty of 1747.

Walk from the car park on to and past Inverlochlarig (the name means the mouth of the loch of the pass) House. Remember to shut any gates you may open.

A Land Rover track leads westwards up the glen. Look out for a prominent wooden bridge and cross the river about one mile west of Inverlochlarig.

Go uphill by steep and sometimes rocky slopes by following the burn flowing from the *bealach* (pass) east of the main top and called Bealach Coire an Laoigh (the pass of the corrie of the calves). Laoigh is pronounced Looee.

The top is rocky, but with care is easily reached.

The wide views include Ben A'n, Ben Lomond, Ben Venue, Ben Ledi, and most of the Crianlarich and

Tyndrum Hills. Ben Dòrain at Bridge of Orchy can be seen, and the southern ends of Beinn a' Chroin and Beinn Chabhair emphasise the lonely character of this piece of country which even the Land Rover track does not spoil.

Look out for good views down to Loch Katrine and west to the lower hills near the north end of Loch Lomond.

It is tempting, as one drives the length of Balquhidder Glen and admires the shape of Stob a' Choin above the waters of Loch Doine, to plan to go up it by way of the eastern shoulders which swing north and slope down towards Blaircreich, but there are problems.

It means going through the grounds of Blaircreich Farm—a former MacGregor holding—to get across the Allt Sgionie at that point on to its western bank, so do ask permission.

If going south up Glen Sgionie, before turning west up on to the shoulder remember there is now no bridge up that glen. The spars of a ruined structure were there at the time of writing but are not recommended.

If the burn is low it is easy to ford.

When you proceed along the knolly ridge towards the main top (you strike an old fence on the crest of the shoulder) watch out for an early view of Loch Katrine.

When you near the final dip of the Bealach Coire an Laoigh, contour the last high mound on its southern side to reach the dip without unnecessary 'up-and-downing'.

Stob a' Choin is an attractive hill, but its twisting character and very steep sides make it one for the experienced hill-walker. In mist, great care is needed to avoid the bluffs.

Walk 18: The Pass of the Dead (Bealach nan Corp), 14 miles, hill-crossing from Inverlochlarig, Balquhidder, to Glen Gyle, Loch Katrine, and back. O.S. sheets 56 and 57.

This walk can give an impressive feeling of wilderness, but it is one for the fit and experienced hill-walker as the going is rough and wet in places. A shortened version can also be achieved provided one has transport at the far end.

Basically, this walk takes one back to one's starting point at Inverlochlarig where Rob Roy MacGregor died in 1734.

Perhaps more than any other walk in the Trossachs it can give the flavour of the old MacGregors, the Children of the Mist, holding on tenaciously to their mountain fastnesses. It goes through some lonely territory where grass-covered mounds and stone 'outlines' tell of once flourishing townships and shielings.

Dorothy and William Wordsworth, and their friend, the poet Coleridge, were at Glen Gyle, Loch Katrine, in 1803 and probably used this pass on 13th September to reach Balquhidder. James Hogg, the Ettrick Shepherd, also visited Glen Gyle.

The history of the Bealach nan Corp—the Pass of the Dead—at the head of the glen, five miles beyond Inverlochlarig, is a matter of some conjecture. One theory says it is where the MacGregors carried back their dead after a fight in Glen Falloch following a reiving expedition. It is more likely, however, that it was the normal route taken for MacGregor funerals. There used to be cairns by the side of the track where the bearers would halt and rest the coffins.

The MacGregors of Glencarnaig had their own burial ground, but those at the head of Loch Doine took their dead over to Loch Katrineside for burial, and some over to Loch Lomondside.

The old townships of north and south Drumlich in the glen near and past the peak of Stob a' Choin would provide bearers and resting places. The remains of these now vanished places of habitation can still be seen.

The present-day walker will see deer and sheep where cattle once grazed, but when among the boulders, the heather slopes, the peat bogs and the steep sides of the surrounding mountains, it is not hard to imagine bowed tartan-clad figures carrying their dead over the prominent *bealach.*

To get to your starting point, drive along the A.84 to Kingshouse and then drive the length of Balquhidder Glen to near Inverlochlarig. Just before the houses, and at a junction, is the stone shelter and picnic place erected by Stirling District Council. Park there.

As you pass the houses at Inverlochlarig you are leaving the site of Rob Roy's death for that of his birth, for he was the son of Donald MacGregor of Glen Gyle.

You pass (left) a brown harled house and an old steading which surely had its foundations in Rob Roy's time.

The MacGregors carrying their dead over the Bealach nan Corp.

On your right are the Munro-tops of Beinn Tulaichean (3,099 feet) and beyond it the prow-top of Cruach Ardrain (3,428 feet).

You pass a white-walled house and a petrol pump and then turn *left* through a white gate, following the track.

You then cross a bridge over the Inverlochlarig Burn, and pass between two white farm buildings and through another gate.

A Land Rover track (not on the map the full way) runs up the glen for about four miles, with the steep sides of the Stob a' Choin overlooking it (left) and the end nose of Beinn a' Chroin (mountain of the cloven hoof) (3,104 feet) on your right.

A glance to the north, just before totally passing the south end of Beinn Tulaichean, gives a good view up Inverlochlarig Glen to Stob Binnein (3,821 feet), looking very much like a sharp pointed peak, hence one interpretation of its name (Stob an Binnein) and very unlike the flat, sawn-off-top view you get from the A.84, which demonstrates the other interpretation, Stob Inneoin, the anvil hill.

You reach an old sheep fank (pen) where a prominent burn, the Ishag, comes down on your right from the corrie between Beinn Tulaichean and Stob Glas. Traces of the old track can be seen here and there.

You go through another gate just past the fank— keep a look out for the stone remains of the townships and old shielings.

You pass through another gate and will see on your left (not on the map) the bridge across the main burn which leads to Stob a' Choin. Continue your journey west on the Land Rover track.

BALQUHIDDER

As you pass Stob a' Choin you will see a prominent dip between it and its western neighbour, Stob an Duibhe. That is the way you will return to this glen from Loch Katrineside.

More townships and shieling ruins are passed, and very fine views can be had by turning round and looking down the beautifully shaped funnel of the glen to the distant lochs of Doine and Voil.

Just past the 'return dip' you will see on the left of your path some prominent boulders which are good for a snack-stop.

You then reach a round corrugated-sheeted sheep fank, which is as ugly as the stone structures are attractive, and here the broad track ends.

An intermittent track wends its way over rough ground to the ridge ahead where the *bealach* will soon be clearly identified. More shieling ruins can be seen, and the path vanishes from time to time.

Follow the burn due west and pass through a gate and an old fence. Follow the fence beside the burn.

The wild Coire a' Chuilinn is on your right and the southern end of Beinn a' Chroin, with An Caisteal, 3,265 feet (pronounced An Has-chul, the castle), further back. Beinn Chabhair, 3,053 feet (pronounced Ca-bar, mountain of the antler), can also be seen.

It is a wild and beautiful corner.

At a junction of the burns leave the fence and take the left fork. There are some more shieling remains here, and good views back down the glen with one prominent boulder in mid-glen looking like something out of *Kidnapped.*

Cross the burn over rough ground with the fence now close to your right, and the knoll ahead with the *bealach* to its left is unmistakable.

Go through a gate in the fence, cross boggy ground and make for a prominent boulder with the notch of the *bealach* beyond it.

The *bealach* itself is broad and boggy and you look down into Glen Gyle (*goill*, forked) and a line of pylons!

A broad gully leads between some rocky sections down to a track at the foot of the pylons. Follow the track down the glen, crossing through a gate, over a bridge, through another gate and across a bridge which has a notice (once you are over) saying 'dangerous bridge'.

The boggy track crosses some sections made up of greasy sleepers and ends on the Lower Clyde Water Board's metalled road which runs from Loch Katrine pier round to Stronachlachar. This is a private road so you can not be picked up by car at this point, but those wanting to end the walk here should turn right and tramp the three miles to Stronachlachar (*Sron a' Chlachair*, stonemason's point) where a car can await you, having been driven in from Aberfoyle on the B.829.

To continue the full route back to Inverlochlarig turn *left* and follow the metalled road past Glen Gyle House and pleasant pine woods.

This is a historic spot although nowadays the reservoir loch is twelve–fifteen feet higher than in Rob Roy's time, and the road, pylons, and modern houses make old tales of a water bull in Loch Katrine sound very ancient. But the water and the shores are still lovely and it is worth a halt.

Dorothy Wordsworth left a pleasant account of her stay with the family at Glen Gyle House, and there was an old township nearby called Kilnacallich which may have been the site of a community of nuns.

The site of Glen Gyle House is very old, and it was the home of the chieftains of that branch of the Clan MacGregor.

The MacGregors did not miss many fights and in the 1715 Jacobite Rising the Glen Gyle contingent were led by Gregor Black Knee, Rob Roy and MacGregor of Balhaldie (near Dunblane).

In the '45 they were led by Robert MacGregor of Glencarnaig who commanded them at the Battle of Prestonpans and on the march to Derby. He later migrated to America and fell during the American War of Independence.

Follow the metalled road round to Portnellan (*port an eilein*, harbour of the island) where the MacGregors buried their dead and where their burial place has been rescued from the loch-reservoir and resited on a little promontory.

Just opposite Black Island a large burn, the Allt a' Choin, comes down and passes under the road. This is your route back. Watch out for some pens at this spot, with gates at a junction of fences. Take the right gate and follow the line of the burn-gorge uphill. You pass through another gate. The ground levels off and it is a good place for a breather with good views across Loch Katrine to the houses at Stronachlachar. Ben Lomond starts to come into view across the intervening glens.

The burn comes from a lochan at the west end of Stob a' Choin, about two and a half miles away.

The first part of this section is heaven, the next can be purgatory! The burn has many beautiful pools but as one nears the lochan the 'flats' can become very boggy and wet. Stick to the fence, but at some times of the year there will be nothing for it but to grimace and splash on. Why the MacGregors did not use this way as their 'coffin route' is clear.

A word of warning—when going up the Allt a' Choin do not be tempted, after a quick look at the map, to deviate to the Bealach Coire an Laoigh on the east side of Stob a' Choin and just below its top. It is the pass of the calves (deer), and is not a traditional human's pass.

When near the lochan, cross the burn to the right and go through a gate. Just before the drop down again to the main Balquhidder Glen you pass another prominent boulder which can give good shelter.

Follow the main glen burn down on its right (south) bank until you can see the lowest point of the Land Rover track across the burn and then cross (paddle, wade) over to it. If the burn is in spate stick to the near (south) bank until you reach the bridge you passed on your way up the glen. Follow the Land Rover track back to Inverlochlarig.

Walk mainly

linked to

Strathyre

Walk 19: Beinn an t-Sithein (1,852 feet), Hill of the Fairies, 3½ miles round, or less depending on choice, from Strathyre, A.84. O.S. sheet 57.

The name Strathyre puzzles some people because, as one drives up or down the busy A.84 between Callander and Lochearnhead, it looks like a narrow pass and not a broad strath.

Yet once you cross the old bridge over the River Balvag you see the valley clearly broaden out. In the eighteenth century the cattle drovers rested and watered their beasts on the meadows. The name may derive from Strath-Eireann, the strath of Ireland, a link with early Celtic Churchmen. It was spelled Strathyire in 1457.

It is an area packed with history. Beinn an t-Sithein (pronounced Ben an Shee-an) is a marvellous viewpoint. It makes a pleasant and leisurely family outing.

Many sharply defined mound-shaped hills are called fairy hills—Schiehallion at Loch Rannoch, Ben Tee, Lochaber, or Ben Tee in the Ochils. Do not scoff too readily (see Walk 21, Doon Hill, Aberfoyle).

STRATHYRE

Present-day Strathyre is built on the site of an old crofting community which vanished when the railway (since gone) came almost a century ago.

It was the birthplace in 1716 of Dugald Buchanan, Gaelic scholar, poet and evangelist: a monument to him is in the centre of the village.

Strathyre has been a Forestry Commission Centre since the 1930s, and distinguished visitors passing through in yester-year included the Wordsworths in 1803. Dorothy and William found lodgings there on the evening of 13th September after they had tramped over the hills from Loch Katrine to Balquhidder.

One of the best-known Scottish songs is entitled 'Bonnie Strathyre', but to see 'the peak of Ben Vorlich girdled by fire', as one verse has it, you have to climb out of the Strath on to Beinn an t-Sithein. (Sung quickly, the song sounds suspiciously like a dance tune called 'The Muckin' o' Geordie's Byre'.)

To climb the hill, cross the old bridge and you will find on the right a pleasant car park and shop called The Trading Post which also serves coffee and refreshments.

Just past the St John's holiday home for the blind (left) you come to a road junction.

The right branch follows an ancient route to Balquhidder. The left terminates at Laggan Farm, on Loch Lubnaigside.

It is intriguing to note that parts of this road were built by soldiers—by General Wade's men in the eighteenth century and by Italian prisoners of war during the Second World War.

Go *left*: a few yards along, a signposted track goes uphill (blue markers for Beinn an t-Sithein).

You reach a forestry road (no signs, at time of writing). Go *right*. You will soon see another sign and a pole with blue, green and yellow markings which take you uphill.

(For those who are fit and who do not like way-marking there is a very steep gap in the trees which takes the walker straight up and down.)

Another forest road is reached: one branch (green)—a forest walk—goes off right to Bailefuill. Go uphill again by a path (blue markers) through whispering trees and you eventually get clear and (right) on to the open hillside, where an easily followed path takes you to the top of the knoll.

The view is stupendous. Take care when going to the front (east) of the knoll: it falls away steeply. Loch Lubnaig spreads out below: on the marshy flats where the River Balvag enters once stood an ancient crannog. The area between Loch Voil and Loch Lubnaig tends to flood although, five miles away, Loch Voil is only seventeen feet higher, and it was along 'Balvaig's swampy course' that Scott depicted the Fiery Cross being carried in *The Lady of the Lake*.

Rob Roy escaped from the Duke of Montrose's soldiers in the area between Strathyre and Balquhidder after being taken prisoner.

To the east the tops of Ben Vorlich, Stuc a' Chroin and Beinn Each show prominently.

To the south, Ardnandave Hill and Ben Ledi also catch the eye. At the back, the steep sides of Benvane and Glen Buckie, and the pass to Brig o' Turk, Stob a' Choin, Stob Binnein, Ben More, Ben Lawers and its neighbours, all show clearly. Loch Earn can be seen, and the Braes of Balquhidder, and much of Strathyre. The front of the knoll cuts off some of the view.

You can descend the way you came, but experienced hill-walkers might want to complete the round by descending the long northern shoulder over Buachaill Breige (the false shepherd) and reaching the Glen Buckie road near the old Stewart holding of Gartnafuaran, then walking round and back to Strathyre. Once on the road you pass, in turn, Stroneslaney where the MacLarens' and Buchanans' fierce thirteenth-century clash occurred, Bailefuill, and the large house of Ardoch (the high field).

Walks mainly

linked to

Aberfoyle

Walk 20: Highland Edge Walk, 5 miles, 3 hours, from Braeval car park and return, 1 mile east of Aberfoyle, A.81. O.S. sheet 57.

Considering its situation at the junction of glens and passes the village of Aberfoyle was never of major strategic importance.

The reason was that warring armies crossed the Forth nearer Stirling at the famous Fords of Frew. Aberfoyle is sited just below the meeting-place of two streams that form the Forth, the Duchray Water from the eastern slopes of Ben Lomond and the Avon-Dhu (black water) from Loch Ard.

But it has an interesting pedigree for all that and this walk, taking in Lime Craig at 1,000 feet is a splendid introduction to the Trossachs from this side. It has breathtaking views.

From Braeval car park the Forestry Commission have way-marked the route (*silver rings* on posts) along forest tracks.

To gain a wilderness-experience you have to shut

your eyes to such signs as 'no articulated lorries' and the fire-watch hut and the TV-relay masts on top of Lime Craig but nothing can spoil the view over the forests and the lower ground. Highlanders in past centuries scanned the trails from here, seeking early warning of the movement of the Redcoat soldiers.

As you ascend, Aberfoyle village appears and disappears in the trees. The name means mouth of the muddy pool (*abar a'phuill*).

The original clachan (from *clach*, standing stones) of Aberfoyle was Kirkton, easily seen over the young Forth, and the other older part, Milton (township of the mill) lies along the Inversnaid road.

Aberfoyle was once the centre of an iron-smelting industry, and it also saw many clansmen on their way to war. The Glen Gyle MacGregors marched through in the 1745 Jacobite Rising, showing off to the Aberfoyle girls and later occupying Doune Castle where Hanoverian prisoners were kept.

Walter Scott, of course, drew on fact when he portrayed its inns as a mecca for the clansmen in the glens round about, and the Bailie Nicol Jarvie Hotel draws its name from his novel *Rob Roy*. The fictional Bailie set a Highlander's plaid on fire with a red-hot coulter (plough blade). Scott jotted down his preliminary notes for *Rob Roy* in the manse of Aberfoyle. Another literary connection is the Jacobite poet, William Glen, who was born near here and who wrote the song 'Wae's me for Prince Charlie'. Queen Victoria gave Aberfoyle a favourable mention in her diary on 2nd September 1869. In near-modern times it once had a railway serving its slate quarries, and was also the centre for Walt Disney's film *Rob Roy, the Highland Rogue.*

The walk up poses no difficulty, and from the top of Lime Craig one can see to the south the Fintry Hills and the whole line of the Campsies, and on the flat ground the trees, marsh and farms on the now partially drained ground of the Flanders Moss, one of the most strategically significant wildernesses in Scotland.

The name does *not* derive from the fact that mosses were used as padding for bandages in Flanders, but probably from a Scots word meaning shaking or trembling, or possibly from an old word 'flinders' meaning fragments of wood. In 1767 Lord Kames of Blair Drummond gave landless men the opportunity to clear part of the moss of peat and to found homes and create small farms. Flemish settlers from Northern Belgium also helped to reclaim the moss which has given rise to another theory for the origin of the name Flanders (but the name is older).

You only see a portion of it, but it is a truly fringe Highland view of importance.

Its bogs and marshes once covered the flood-plain of the upper Forth, from Aberfoyle almost to Stirling, an area of fifty square miles.

It is sometimes said that the Romans cut down the original woods to make causeways or to flush out enemies, but it may be that the boggy marsh simply killed off the trees and prevented regeneration.

In the narrow waist of Scotland the bogs were of major strategic significance—hence the vital importance of Stirling Bridge, the first major crossing point after the Forth becomes wide.

Rob Roy and his men knew local tracks over the marshes and offered to lead the Jacobite Army across in 1715, but the opportunity was not seized.

The Lime Craig view takes in the wooded hills and glens of the 42,000 acres that make up the Queen Elizabeth Forest Park which is run by the Forestry Commission. The David Marshall Lodge, a visitor and information centre, sits on its knoll. It was gifted to the Commission in 1960 and is named after a former Trust chairman.

Beyond is an old slate quarry and the slopes of Ben Venue. The Duke's Pass or Road is almost totally hidden by trees here.

The Glen Finglas reservoir, Benvane and Ben Ledi, can also be seen. In front of Ben Ledi, Loch Drunkie shows up clearly, and further round is the back of the Menteith Hills. Rob Roy raided the farm at Drunkie for provisions during the 1719 Jacobite Rising, which took place mainly in the north-west Highlands. The line of the Highland Boundary Fault is clearly apparent, and the combination of hills, moors, lochs and forests is entrancing.

Those who do not like steep ground should go back the way they came.

The way-marked path descends over muddy and steep ground to the woods. The second half is duller, a plod through the trees and passing in succession the lime quarry which give the hill its name (left), the David Marshall Lodge paths (right), an old cottage (left), Dounans school camp grounds and Aberfoyle golf course (right) before returning to Braeval car park.

Walk 21: Doon Hill, Aberfoyle, 1 mile, stroll. O.S. sheet 57.

It is all too easy nowadays to scoff at fairies, but it is a serious subject and should not be lightly discussed. In any case, Gaelic fairies were not seen as slim girls with long gossamer wings, like extras in *A Midsummer Night's Dream*, but mysterious little people, both male and female, some malevolent and some helpful.

Kirkton, the original clachan of Aberfoyle, lies to the south of the modern village and over the narrow bridge which spans the infant Forth.

The Reverend Robert Kirk, Gaelic scholar and investigator of faery lore, ministered there and at Balquhidder until his death in 1692.

His mortal remains are buried in Aberfoyle, but it is said he was spirited away by fairies while walking on the Faery Knowe, or Doon Hill, the year after he wrote a book about their life-patterns entitled *The Secret Commonwealth of Elves, Fauns and Fairies.* A pine tree on top of wooded Doon Hill is called 'The Minister's Pine' and is said to mark the spot of his removal and contain his spirit.

The hill also has older associations. Aedan, Prince of the Forth (A.D. 570–604), of the Scots kingdom of Dalriada, is reputed to have had a fort (Eperpuill) at Doon Hill.

It is a Forestry Commission way-marked route so if you want to sense it as people must have felt about it long ago, go in the early morning or late evening or even out of season.

Drive to the small car park at Balleich on Manse Road, south from Aberfoyle. The half-mile circular

trail, marked by 'toadstool' signs, leads to the summit (and the pine) and back again.

Walk 22: The Menteith Hills (1,320 feet), 2½ miles, high-level walk on the edge of the Highlands, from Braeval car park (see Walk 20). O.S. sheet 57.

This is a most marvellous viewpoint on a clear day, easily reached, and dazzingly attractive when the heather is in bloom.

Two of the most popular ways in the past of getting to the highest point are now inadvisable.

The heather-clad, knolly hills run north-east from Braeval to Loch Venachar and it is tempting to make the crossing by the pass at their foot, to turn uphill at the north-east end and return to Braeval along the crest of the hills. But the heather is very long and tussocky and the north-east end is now 'ditched' and planted with trees. Do not try it.

In any event, the highest point, marked 400 metres (1,320 feet) on the map, is at the south-west end.

Also resist the temptation to turn sharp left after leaving the woods at Braeval and to turn uphill to a prominent cleft or notch. The way is now closed off by barbed wire but was the favourite route to the top in past years.

But that is enough carping. The hill can be ascended from the Lime Craig walk and also from the David Marshall Lodge.

The Reverend Robert Kirk, Gaelic scholar, minister and author of faery lore.

Here, indeed, we have a frontier hill.

R. B. Cunninghame-Graham, (1852–1936), popularly known as 'Don Roberto', the nineteenth-century Scots aristocrat, adventurer, writer, M.P., South American explorer and gaucho, descendant of Robert the Bruce, Laird of Gartmore, political pioneer, and much else besides, wrote:

'Perhaps no district of the Highland frontier was so typically a borderland as the District of Menteith: perhaps at no point in all Scotland is the dividing line between Celt and Saxon more distinct in the nomenclature of language and configuration of the two countries.'

We are on the verge here of that dominating geological feature, the Highland Boundary Fault.

The straths and fields to the south are part of the belt of Lower Old Age Sandstone which crosses all Scotland diagonally. The mountains are massed formations of hard quartzites and schists with some knobs of diorite and granite.

The contrasts are startling and the views are superlative.

Scott wrote in *The Lady of the Lake*:

> The noble stag was pausing now,
> Upon the mountain's southern brow,
> Where broad extended, far beneath,
> The varied realms of fair Menteith.

Take the Lime Craig walk route from Braeval until just before the forest road swings left in a big curve where you then see ahead of you the tree-filled glen-gap carved out by the burn.

At this point keep a *very sharp* eye out at the right-hand side of the 'road'. What looks like a *small*, muddy little dried-up burn or cutting appears. A few feet up it becomes a path, churned up by the hooves of pony-trekking ponies.

It is very hard to spot in its early stage, but it soon turns into a recognisable path going up the right-hand side of the burn (as you face up).

You go through a gate and the path winds its way up the hillside. It has off-shoots, but keep going high. You go up in steep zig-zags, then reach the top of a hill with good views over the lower ground.

Not long afterwards you see the hut on the top of Lime Craig to your left and the path swings along the hillside. You will soon see ahead of you the white trig point on the highest top.

The hills are deep in heather. Just before the final mound the path loses itself in a dip but stay high and the final top will easily be found. There is a rusty fence nearby.

Return the way you came: there are other variations but it is easy to go wrong. You may be bothered by flies in some sections of this walk in the summer as they are attracted by the horse dung.

To the east, you see far off the Ochils and nearby the Lake of Menteith. The castle rock at Stirling and the Wallace Monument can be seen. Moving round to the south the Gargunnock, Fintry and Campsie Hills (and the prominent hill of Dumgoyne) are also in sight. Flanders Moss is clearly viewed. Over the way is Beinn Dearg and Ben Gullipen and beyond one can see the mounds of Uamh Mhór and Uamh Bheag, Ben Vorlich, Stuc a' Chroin, Beinn Each, Loch Venachar, Ben Ledi, Benvane, the wooded mouth of Glen Finglas and its reservoir. Ben More and Stob Binnein at Crianlarich are also visible and, moving westwards, Beinn Tulaichean and Cruach Ardrain, and the peaks at the head of Loch Lomond, Beinn a' Chroin, An Caisteal and Beinn Chabhair can be seen. Loch Katrine and Ben A'n are prominent, and hidden Loch Drunkie and its neighbouring woods are close by. Behind Ben Lomond one can see the Cobbler and its neighbours at Arrochar.

The Lake of Menteith spreads attractively out.

Visitors are sometimes intrigued as to why the Lake of Menteith is not called Loch. One theory is that it is from an old Scots word 'laigh' meaning low-lying, but the explanation is straightforward. It has been anglicised on some maps and in some writings, and Lake has stuck. The Ordnance Survey of 1860, and Queen Victoria in 1869, both used the word Loch.

The island of Inchmahome contains the ruins of a priory to which Mary Queen of Scots, as a child, was sent in September 1547 for safety from the invading armies of Henry VIII of England who wanted to coerce the Scots into agreeing to arrange a marriage with Prince Edward. The invasion was known as the Rough Wooing.

The monastery was authorised by a Papal document as early as 1238.

The island was the burying ground of the Grahams. Another island, Inch Tulla, was an ancient stronghold of the Earls of Menteith.

It is intriguing to note that this loch, not Loch Katrine or Loch Achray, might have been the setting for *The Lady of the Lake.*

Sir Walter called on William MacGregor Stirling, historian and minister at Port of Menteith, and discovered he was writing a poem called 'Inchmahome' and this reputedly caused Sir Walter to switch the scene of his own poem to Loch Katrine.

106

The Department of the Environment runs a boat service to the island which is popular with tourists. The loch has also been the scene of some spectacular gatherings in winter when thousands have gathered on the ice to play the ancient game of curling.

Walk 23: Braeval, Aberfoyle, to Callander, 7 miles, easy hill-pass crossing, off the A.81. O.S. sheet 57.

Menteith (properly, Mon-teith, the mouth or watershed of the River Teith) was formerly one of the great territories of Scotland. It stretched to over 200 square miles and was once an important earldom.

The name nowadays tends to be applied only to the area around the Lake of Menteith.

It is a name with sorrowful connotations in Scottish history because Sir John Stewart, uncle and tutor of the young Earl of Menteith, is alleged to have handed over the Scottish guerrilla leader, William Wallace, to the conquering English in 1305 (Robert Bruce, however, is said to have forgiven him and he fought on Bruce's side in the Scottish Wars of Independence). It is only fair to say that some historians vehemently deny that Sir John Stewart betrayed Wallace.

This walk, running through the hills from near Aberfoyle to Callander and parallel to the Menteith Hills, is an attractive hill-pass crossing, of great antiquity, and was undoubtedly used during these turbulent centuries. It parallels a Roman route.

It poses no difficulties, and is way-marked.

Beyond Braeval, about a mile (east) out of Aberfoyle on the A.81 the Forestry Commission have built a car park and marked a woodland walk. Watch out for the sign on the left after passing Aberfoyle golf course. Braeval means 'the slope of the township'.

The route is also way-marked with posts (black chevrons if you are going the whole way to Callander and white/silver if you are doing the woodland walk).

The first stretch is a broad Forestry Commission track with, at the end of attractive plantations, a gate and stile, and a drystane dyke. (The way-marking posts at this point also have a yellow mark on the reverse for people coming from Callander to Aberfoyle.)

Looking back from the stile, one can see the Campsies and the Fintry Hills, tantalising early glimpses of good views to come.

Keep going on pleasant moorland walking, with good views of Beinn Dearg (the red mountain) and Ben Gullipen (right) (the mountain of the curlew) until you reach another drystane dyke, this time with a gate that one opens and closes.

The moorland becomes wilder with thick bracken and heather, but the path is clear. Another dyke is passed, and just over the crest of the pass and the drop to the Callander side there are fine views of Ben Ledi's steep south-west sides, with the tips of Stuc a' Chroin and Ben Vorlich, the two Munros at Loch Earn, clearly showing above the hills ahead.

Forestry drainage on the hillsides has resulted in a small lochan being born (not shown on the map) and the path is crossed by a forestry track at the end of this lochan.

Go carefully *across* this track and you will pick up the path descending to Loch Venachar. Do *not* go east along a forest 'road'. The waters of the loch stretch out beautifully, and the higher buildings of Callander can now be seen.

As one descends to the loch an exquisitely attractive view opens out with Ben Ledi, green and dominating, across the way, and woods, moor and fields. To the left, Ben A'n can be seen, a pointed rocky peak above Loch Katrine.

The knolly top of Ben Venue also appears on the left, and on a good day this is one of the most pleasant views in the Trossachs area.

Loch Venachar (the pointed loch) has a monster, an old Gaelic tale of a water horse who invited children to ride on its back and then drowned them. A woodland area on the north shore, called Coille a' Bhròin, has been translated as 'wood of sorrow' and is linked to this story.

In modern times, warnings are regularly issued to visitors that many Scottish lochs shelve steeply after initial shallows. The water, even in summer, can be very cold and easily causes cramp.

At the west end of the loch the MacGregors used to have a gathering place. Sir Walter Scott wrote in *The Lady of the Lake*:

> The muster-place is Lanrick mead;
> Speed forth the signal! clansmen, speed!

He depicted the marshy flat ground at the head of the loch as the muster-place of Roderick Dhu's clansmen.

Sir Walter, when staying at Cambusmore, rode from Loch Venachar to Stirling Castle to see if he was being accurate in the time he had assigned to Fitz-James' grey horse, Bayard, in the appropriate stanza of *The Lady of the Lake* after the duel with Roderick Dhu.

The crossing path eventually ends at the Invertrossachs road near West Dullater. You drop steeply down a good path to the tarmac road at the lochside.

Remember that this a private road so if you are being picked up by car you will have to seek permission to drive along it. You can, however, walk past East Lodge where, further along the lochside, your pick-up car can await you at a pre-arranged spot.

You can walk into Callander if you wish on tarmac roads, fairly busy with tourist traffic but, if you want to retain the flavour of the crossing, end it as soon as possible after descending to the road.

Some walkers prefer to walk on the lochside road past the east end of the loch and its dam to a junction with the A.892, then turn sharp left (north-west) across an attractive bridge over the River Leny to the A.821 and be picked up by car there.

Walk 24: Craigmore (1,258 feet), Aberfoyle, short hill-pound for the fit. O.S. sheet 57.

Craigmore (the big rock or crag), with its steep quarry face, is very prominent above Aberfoyle, or from the A.821 Duke's Road or Pass between Aberfoyle and Loch Katrine, and is clearly seen from many other points.

It gives reasonable views, particularly to Loch Ard and to many otherwise hidden corners of the area.

The old Aberfoyle slate quarries, once the third largest in Scotland, lie half a mile to the north.

The MacGregors used Craigmore as a look-out or signal point.

It dominates the pass to Loch Ard which ultimately goes on to Inversnaid on Loch Lomondside, and overlooks the Duchray Water.

In Sir Walter's day there was tourist traffic between Kinlochard and Rowardennan on Loch Lomond along a track which ran west from the Duchray Water. Tourists, escorted by guides, rode on ponies.

Across the road from Craigmore is the David Marshall Lodge and the old Trossachs drove road.

The Pass of Aberfoyle was the scene of fierce clashes in 1651 when General Monk, Cromwell's military commander in Scotland, tried to subdue the royalist clans.

They were again active here in 1653–4 when the Earl of Glencairn organised a Rising. Monk's men were ambushed in the pass and routed by soldiers and clansmen led by Glencairn and Graham of Duchray, whose castle was burned.

The easiest way up Craigmore is to leave your car at the David Marshall Lodge car park. Leave the road entrance, turn right, cross the road (watch for traffic) and look out for a track on the left (west) of the road, at a bend, going steeply uphill.

After a bit you reach a 'road' going to the prominent quarry on the south face of Craigmore.

Cross the 'road' and continue uphill. Cross a fence (stile). The path in sections is built up, a relic of the quarry days. You will see another track, leading to the quarries further up the Duke's Road, but continue uphill.

On the top mound, follow a track with a deer fence and forestry plantations on your right (north).

On the highest mound of Craigmore there is a cairn a short way down from the top but nothing on the actual summit except the remnants of an old post.

The Aberfoyle quarries lie ahead to the north, and the hummocky ridge leading to Ben Venue over Creag Innich and Beinn an Fhògharaidh is clearly seen. This is a route to the summit of Ben Venue sometimes used by walkers setting out from Aberfoyle.

It is worth going to the south edge of Craigmore to see the view from there.

Descend the same way as you came up but if you follow the line of the fence down you should eventually see another stile which leads into the plantations and the line of the old tramway which once linked the quarry with the old railway station in Aberfoyle. The track-line is marked on the map.

Do not go into the plantations, though, merely use the stile as a marker for a faint and steep track from it which runs south-east downhill and crosses a fence where there are two stiles side by side.

This track reaches the Duke's Road at a bend where there is a pull-in point on the other side, litter-bins and a nearby seat, all overlooking the David Marshall Lodge. Again, keep a sharp look out for traffic on the road.

The Aberfoyle quarries are large but much of the piled slate is in a dangerous condition and it is no place for the casual visitor.

The old slate remnants are steep, piled high, frequently loose and some sections are ready to slide, particularly after wet weather.

On a ridge above the quarries are a number of cairns which mark the site of a bloody clash between some Lochaber cattle reivers and men from Lennox and Menteith who caught up with them.

A temptation to walk up the Duke's Road or Pass to the eastern entrance of the quarries and to return by the line of the tramway should be resisted. The woods are pleasant, but the north sections of the line are broken up by tiny 'canyons' caused by quarrying which mean some scrambling and could cause difficulty for elderly or unsure walkers.

Craigmore's views are slightly disappointing for such a prominent crag but it does have a good prospect of Ben Lomond, over the nearby lochs and towards the Lodge.

Those who like Cunninghame-Graham's writings will see that the map shows near the summit of the Duke's Road, a small loch, Lochan Reoidhte, the frozen or icy loch. It is now screened by trees, but 'Don Roberto' mentioned it in his book *Notes On the District of Menteith*.

Walk 25: Ben Venue (2,393 feet), A.821, three walking permutations. O.S. sheet 57.

Ben Venue, hill of the caves (or possibly mountain of milk or of the young cattle, *a'bheinn mheanbh*) is one of the finest hills in the Trossachs, with its twin tops and western outliers making it easily seen from afar off.

To the north and north-east it is steep, craggy and knolly and after rain there are many waterfalls. It is a truly beautiful hill.

The sides bordering Loch Katrine contain the Bealach nam Bo, the Pass of the Cattle, a trade route in past centuries for cattle going to the Falkirk Tryst and a back-door for beasts 'lifted' by the MacGregors.

Here, too, is the black chasm or gully known as Coire na Urisgean, Goblin's Corrie or Cave, where shadowy, supernatural life-sized beings are reputed to have lived.

Sir Walter Scott wrote in *The Lady of the Lake*:

> High on the south, huge Benvenue
> Down on the lake in masses threw
> Crags, knolls and mounds, confusedly hurl'd,
> The fragments of an earlier world.

Scott depicted the Goblin's Corrie or Cave as a retreat for Ellen Douglas and her father after they had withdrawn from Roderick Dhu's stronghold on an island in Loch Katrine.

There are normally three main ways to the top, and the views over the woods and lochs of the Trossachs are marvellous.

Drive to the Loch Achray Hotel: if you travel via the Duke's Road or Pass it is worth recalling that the Duke of Montrose had a road made over the ancient tracks because of the large numbers of tourists attracted by Sir Walter Scott's writings. Landowners were responsible for many of the oak trees you see: the bark was used for tanning. The woods are natural oak in the main and were also used in the making of charcoal. They were supervised and 'cropped' and there was replacement planting.

If you come from Callander, look out for an attractive old church (left) on a knoll overlooking Loch Achray. It is dedicated to the Celtic St Kessog who preached the Gospel as early as A.D. 525, before St Columba landed on Iona and before St Augustine reintroduced Christianity to the southern half of Britain.

Dorothy Wordsworth and Queen Victoria greatly liked Loch Achray, and between Ben Venue and Loch Achray the Stewarts and marauding Campbells fought a fierce engagement during the reign of James I of Scotland.

Sir Walter wrote:

> The Minstrel came once more to view
> The eastern ridge of Benvenue,
> For, ere he parted, he would say
> Farewell to lovely Loch Achray—
> Where shall he find, in foreign land,
> So lone a lake, so sweet a strand!

These last two lines were frequently quoted in tourism literature of yester-year.

The loch, too, was the modern scene of a mountaineering incident which put a new word into the vocabulary of hillmen. Jock Nimlin, former Field Officer of the National Trust for Scotland, pioneer rock climber and one of a hardy band who in the Depression years of the late 1920s walked or hitched long distances to get to the hills, tells how a group were sleeping under an overhang on Loch Achray.

'It was a sort of cave which had been formed perhaps thousands of years earlier when the loch had a higher level. During the 1926 strike miners fed up with no work had gone out into the countryside to fish. They had improved this overhanging section of the bank and put in one or two wooden shores they had collected from driftwood. We soon had a fire going. A tramp came long and he called our shelter a howff.'

The word began to be used by mountaineers and hill-walkers and is now commonly applied to makeshift overnight shelters or caves. ('Howff' is, of course, an old Scots word meaning shelter or abode.)

To ascend the hill from behind Loch Achray Hotel you have a choice of three routes.

The *first* route is the track up Gleann Riabhach, way-marked by the Forestry Commission with blue chevrons.

It follows a corridor between trees and is occasionally badly eroded: a sign eventually swings you right (with a warning notice that you are leaving forest trails for the hill) until you get clear of the trees and into a fine corrie.

You cross a stile and deer fence and the way-marked path takes you up on to the crest of the ridge. The twin tops of Ben Venue are on your right at this stage.

The cliffs of Creag Tharsuinn (cross-shaped or oblique rock) fringe the corrie, and Beinn Bhreac (speckled mountain) can also be seen (see the *third* route).

Way-marking ends at the head of the ridge. The tops of Ben Venue are confusing in mist: there is a dip between the two knolls. You have two options when near the ridge. You can either turn right and pick your own way to the top or get on to the ridge and follow the faint path.

The true but lower top (east knoll) has an old fence post, and a trig point of stones and cement.

The wide view includes Loch Achray and the hotel, the Trossachs Hotel, a flattened out Ben A'n, Loch Venachar, quaintly named Loch Drunkie (ridge of the bank), the Menteith Hills, Ben Ledi, Benvane, Loch Katrine and the long arm of Glen Gyle, the reservoir-loch of Loch Arklet, the hills at the head of Balquhidder, and the Arrochar and Crianlarich Hills. Ben Lomond presents a towering face.

Inexperienced walkers should ascend and descend by Gleann Riabhach. The greatest care must be taken even by experienced walkers in descending the hill to the Loch Katrine sluices or (a *second* choice) by ascending from there via the narrow Pass of Achray. There is no way-marking, the hillside is steep, there are many cliffs and bluffs, and the path marked on the map is faint and vanishes in sections. If you do descend from the Ben to the sluices and are hazy about finding the Pass of Achray track you can take the private road that connects with the A.821 and walk back to the Loch Achray Hotel by the road (beware of traffic).

Much has changed on this side since Scott's day. Where the road to Loch Katrine pier now runs there was once an unbroken defile crossed by a natural ladder using rock ledges and the roots of trees. He wrote in *The Lady of the Lake*:

> Where the rude [rough] Trosachs' dread defile
> Opens on Katrine's lake and isle.

Roderick Dhu's watch-tower was sited on the high rocks on the left as one goes to the pier.

> The summer dawn's reflected hue
> To purple changed Loch Katrine blue;
> Mildly and soft the western breeze
> Just kiss'd the Lake, just stirr'd the trees.

There are dramatic scenes of the MacGregors (Clan Alpine) going to war. So great was its verisimilitude that nineteenth-century visitors argued about details of the stag-hunt and the fighting. Adam Ferguson, serving under Wellington in the Peninsula, received extra rations for reading the poem aloud and on one occasion read the battle scene to keep his company steady while under fire:

> Ben-an's grey scalp the accents knew,
> The joyous wolf from covert drew,
> The exulting eagle scream'd afar—
> They knew the voice of Alpine's war.

And:

> Prompt at the signal of alarms,
> Each son of Alpine rush'd to arms;
> So swept the tumult and affray
> Along the margin of Achray.

It is all stirring stuff which still has a swing to it in modern times.

The *third* route and possibly the most popular (three miles, two and a half hours) is to ascend from Ledard, off the B.829 on the north side of Loch Ard (the high loch).

Ledard Farm, which dates back to the early sixteenth century, is a pony-trekking centre. The farm also has a dairy goat herd.

Immediately behind the farm is the famous Ledard waterfall and pool which Sir Walter brought into his novels *Waverley* and *Rob Roy*.

He stayed at the farm, wrote notes in one of the buildings which can still be seen, and used a rock 'seat' beside the pool to rest, think and write.

It is easy to get on to the wrong side of the burn here so remember that the main path is on the left bank *as you face uphill.*

It is way-marked (green), and follows the side of the Ledard Burn to the gap east of Beinn Bhreac (2,295 feet), and then contours the north slopes of Creag Tharsuinn, working eastwards to the west ridge of Ben Venue (the first route, from Gleann Riabhach, also comes on to this ridge).

People also use this third route to walk from Kinlochard to Brig o' Turk, descending down Gleann Riabhach (the first route in reverse). However, the walk along the tarmac road from the Loch Achray Hotel to Brig o' Turk is not advisable in the tourist season or at weekends because of car and coach traffic.

Ben Venue and Loch Achray, on sunny days, are jewels in the Trossachs crown.

It is worth sitting on a knoll on Ben Venue, or on Ben A'n or near the present-day Trossachs pier and reading *The Lady of the Lake.* Scott depicted the end of the stag chase at the foot of Ben Venue. The sun is setting, the knight is alone. His horse dies and the hounds are recalled. When the echoes of the horn die away, Scott describes the beauties of the woods and hills. Marvellous stuff.

Be it a controversial issue or not you can drive, on a paying basis, into the Achray forest from the Duke's Road (A.821, two and a half miles from Aberfoyle).

There are seven miles of forest road and it includes Loch Drunkie and Loch Achray. For the purposes of this book, it should be said that there are picnic sites, displays, toilets and pleasant walks.

Loch Drunkie was visited by Queen Victoria. Invertrossachs House, where she stayed, was once called Drunkie House but the name, with its unmerited connotations with drinking, was changed for the royal visit. Drunkie is derived from the Gaelic for ridge-of-the-bank.

Walk 26: The Waterfall of the Fawn (or the Grey Mare's Tail), half a mile, David Marshall Lodge, near Aberfoyle. O.S. sheet 57.

This is one of a number of way-marked walks in the Queen Elizabeth Forest Park. It starts at the Lodge car park, is circular, and has signpost displays. In high summer it may be dusty and thronged with people and much of the beauty of the woods and the delicate fall are lost. The display boards are both comprehensive and interesting as an introduction to this part of the area. Those who want a wilderness experience should go out of season or after prolonged rain.

Walk 27: Loch Ard Forest, 6 miles, 3½ hours, silver ring walk, Aberfoyle. O.S. sheet 57.

This is a good-fun, scrambling walk for the energetic

family but contains few outstanding views and has a boring start.

Leave Aberfoyle car park and turn left over the bridge (this is Manse Road). You can miss out this early section by driving along Manse Road to the small Forestry Commission car park at Balleich.

If walking the full way you pass (left) the ruins of the ancient Kirkton church where the Reverend Robert Kirk was buried in 1692 (see Walk 21, Doon Hill) and the scene of an affray in 1671 when the Grahams of nearby Duchray and their distant relatives and followers of the Earl of Airth fell out over, of all things, a christening.

The church was an appendage of Inchmahome Priory on the Lake of Menteith.

At Balleich there is a notice-board giving the various route-marked walks. This one is not on the board but at the side of the track there are silver rings on posts.

A trudge along a tree-fringed tarmac track follows, then on to packed gravel until—at last—a sign turns you right into the woods.

You cross a small bridge and when you eventually emerge at a junction path where there is no way-marker, you turn left.

You then ultimately follow *blue* signs (as well as silver) as this is the latter section of the so-called 'Long Walk' publicised in the A.A.'s *No Through Road.*

The trail becomes mucky in wet weather, and you pass some trees with identification markers—watch out for wood-ant heaps.

The way takes you through part of the Old Duchray (black shieling) estate and past the ruined and gloomy houses of the old township of Daldannet, now shrouded in trees.

Not long after the house of Gartnaul you have a choice of a short cut back to Aberfoyle, or of continuing following the long-walk signs.

The grounds of Duchray Castle are private, but the path takes you downstream along the Duchray Water.

(Part of the castle is sixteenth century and was burned by General Monk in Cromwellian times and also in the '45. Rob Roy was given shelter here on one of his ploys.)

The Duchray Water rises on the northern face of Ben Lomond and is the parent of the River Forth.

You are routed back to Lochan Spling (private fishing) and then back into Aberfoyle.

Not long before you return to the car park, you pass (left) the Covenanters Inn. It is twentieth-, not seventeenth-century, and the name refers to the Scots who gathered there in 1949 to draw up the Scottish Covenant which sought home rule for Scotland and whose petition received two million signatures.

Walk 28: Loch Ard and lochan walk, 3½ miles, 1½ hours, from Milton, Aberfoyle, A.821 and B.829. O.S. sheet 57.

This route gives a beautiful view of that jewel of the Trossachs lochs, Loch Ard, from the opposite side of the water from the busy B.829 to Inversnaid, itself an attractive scenic route.

ABERFOYLE

Ben Lomond dominates its sheltered three-mile length and its wooded and fertile banks make it, like Loch Katrine, a favourite place for botanists.

Queen Victoria sketched it, and Rob Roy MacGregor had a cave on its south bank from which he and his men could watch military traffic through the Pass of Aberfoyle.

Enormous pike have been caught in its waters. Its islands contain an ancient chapel and the ruins of a fifteenth-century stronghold of Murdoch Stewart, Duke of Albany and Earl of Fife.

Drive one mile west of Aberfoyle to Milton (township of the mill). Watch out for a small metalled road going off left which crosses a bridge over the Avon Dhu (black water). An old building with a red post-box faces you at the junction: this is an old mill. This burn-river comes from Loch Ard and further down links with Duchray Water to form the River Forth. Sir Walter Scott drew on reality for his description of the Milton clachan in his novel *Rob Roy*.

Turn sharp *right* up a track signposted 'Youth organisations camp site: Craigmuick Cottage' until you see a Forestry Commission notice outlining way-marked walks and saying 'Craigmuick Cottage'. Take the cottage fork (left) and you will quickly reach a small car park with picnic seats.

Go back to the big signpost and you will see a silver ring post at the side of the track. Follow these posts.

You pass lesser Loch Ard and then get a wide view over Loch Ard itself before returning by woodland tracks, past a small lochan, to your starting point.

On the last stretch back you get a good view of Craigmore (the big rock or crag) above Aberfoyle, Lime Craig and the Menteith Hills.

Walk 29: Milton, Aberfoyle, to Kinlochard, 5½ miles, Forestry Commission way-marked woodland walk (blue). O.S. sheet 57.

This is a pleasant walk alongside Loch Ard with magnificent glimpses of the most impressive face of Ben Lomond.

A way-marked walk (red) for Rowardennan via Ben Lomond at 1,200 feet also leaves from here but is a dullish plod.

The starting point is the same as outlined in the Milton silver ring walk which also starts here.

The silver route goes left at a junction and red and blue goes ahead.

Keep a look out, right, in the latter stages, for the glen above Ledard, on the far side of the loch. Across the loch you can also see Beinn Bhreac and the way up Ben Venue.

You pass through a gate just before you get to Kinlochard proper.

If doing the route in reverse you will see a house called 'Mill of Chon', which the MacGregors used in past centuries.

There is a signposted car park at the forestry houses.

Take care in going back to Milton—the yellow markers (for the return) are obscure at a junction and it is easy to go wrong. If you do, use the loch as a marker—an upper forestry road links with the silver ring walk and also returns to Milton. Remember, blue from Milton to Kinlochard, yellow from Kinlochard to Milton.

Walk 30: Leanach Woodland Walks, 2 miles, 1½ hours, and 5 miles, 2 hours, off Duke's Pass or Road, 3½ miles north of Aberfoyle, A.821. O.S. sheet 57.

Sir Walter Scott loved the woods that hugged the eastern slopes of Ben Venue, and there was a public outcry when they were cut down in the late nineteenth century.

The Forestry Commission have replanted much of the ground with conifers from North America, Europe and Japan, a task begun in the 1940s by prisoners of war and displaced persons.

Just north of the viewpoint knoll of Tom an t-Seallaidh the Commission have built a secluded car park at Leanach (*leantach*—area of the plains) with pleasant views to Ben A'n and the east.

Two way-marked walks are on offer, short (gold rings on posts) and long (silver rings).

The short route crosses the line of an ancient trail from Aberfoyle to the Trossachs and can give something of the flavour of Sir Walter's day.

The longer has some interminable forest 'road' sections with tree 'walls' either side and few vistas. It takes the walker on to the Lòn Mór (the big flat area) where a leaky hut provides a halt-refuge, and then on to the foothills of Ben Venue.

There are some good views of Ben Venue, and a glimpse or two of the Trossachs Hotel.

The short walk (gold) covers part of the route of the long walk (silver). The latter stages of the long walk include the routes of others including the bronze rings of Gleann Riabhach. (*Do not* think you have picked up your short (gold) walk again—both are similar and weather to almost natural shades.) Green is for Brig o' Turk, and blue is for Ben Venue. There is no problem—watch out for your silver rings on the joint posts and, where they break off, for silver only.

Walk 31: Gleann Riabhach, 2 miles, bronze ring walk, Achray Hotel, 5½ miles from Aberfoyle, A.821. O.S. sheet 57.

The title of this route has a prehistoric ring to it but it refers to the coloured band the Forestry Commission has inserted on way-marking poles.

The early sections are pleasant woodland walking, and although the route promises much it never quite matches up to expectations.

It is a good trail, however, for exercising children or a dog.

Go behind the hotel at the west end of Loch Achray and walk along a wide forestry track-road.

Watch out for a post and bronze-painted arrow pointing sharp *left* (just ahead of you on the right will be a similar post but that is for your return). You go up some 'steps'.

The way-marks through the woods are few, thank goodness, and the path is attractive with the glen burn on your left.

At a junction of two tracks, and near a burns' junction, you cross a concrete and metal bridge. The wide track goes left, and you then have to watch out for your bronze arrow pointing *right* where there is a path.

The path is faint for a bit which adds to the

attraction (there is a burn on your left part of the way).

Eventually you hit a wide track-road once again, turn sharp right and will soon have a fine view through a gap in the trees of the turreted Trossachs Hotel, with Ben Ledi lowering behind.

You come back on to a broad track, cross a concrete bridge over the burn, and *pass* a junction-path (blue marker) which goes left to Ben Venue.

Beware of going too far on this broad track: a bronze marker swings you *right* at a point where you can see Ben A'n ahead.

You pass an old sheep fank on both sides of the path, a relic of the days when there were crofting townships and hunting paths in this glen and area, now swallowed by trees.

You come to a junction with a Forestry Commission sign saying 'Brig o' Turk, three miles' (green markers and an unhappy plod on tarmacadam once you reach the road) and 'Trossachs, ½-mile'. You then return on the wide track you first started on.

Walk 32: Ben A'n (1,520 feet), Loch Katrine, 2 miles, hill-walk, 2½ miles, circular (1½ hours), A.821 (T). O.S. sheet 57.

Sir Walter Scott is to blame for calling this pointed peak, so clearly seen from the Duke's Pass or the Duke's Road, Ben A'n.

Its proper name is Am Binnean, the pinnacle, and its situation above the birch woods and modern plantations at the east end of Loch Katrine makes it an attractive viewpoint. It is reputed to be a hill that attracts lightning.

The top is narrow and the path steep and eroded, but it can be ascended without undue difficulty by those able to undertake some scrambling around and who are fit and nimble. It is not a place for the very young, the elderly or the insecure.

Leave the A.821 two hundred yards west of the Trossachs Hotel where a steep path goes up the edge of the woods. *Across* the road (beware of traffic) is a secluded car park. The path is muddy in places, as it ascends through the trees. It levels out at the base of the actual peak where there are fine views to the craggy sides of Ben Venue. When on this level section do not take a faint path going off to the right but stick to the well-beaten track.

Do not be put off by the steep look of the hill, or by the shouts and chit-chat of rock climbers on the crags. The path goes steeply up through a natural dip, clear of the crags, and takes the walker right round the back of the peak.

There is plenty of room just before the top, but the actual summit point is a narrow rock, with room for only two people.

The southern crags are steep, and caution is needed on top.

The length of Loch Katrine, except the arm leading to Glen Gyle, bursts on the eye.

In 1803 the poet Coleridge met his friends William and Dorothy Wordsworth at the shore and it is not surprising that he rushed forward and hailed them with a shout 'exulting in the glory of Scotland'.

Wordsworth, when he was sixty and in ill-health, wrote a sonnet called 'The Trossachs' thirty years after this visit.

You look down on the wooded east end where, during the tourist season, a boat leaves on a sail up the loch to Stronachlachar (*Sron a' Chlachair*, stonemason's point) at the head of the loch, and back to the pier.

In past times, when local oarsmen were making a good living out of rowing tourists up the loch, they objected to a steamboat being brought in. It sank in mysterious circumstances. In the ensuing court case the Highlanders blamed it on a supernatural water bull and concentrated on speaking Gaelic, thus irritating the English-speaking judiciary.

You see, too, Ellen's Isle (originally Eilean Molach, the shaggy isle) on which Sir Walter depicted Roderick Dhu's rustic hall in *The Lady of the Lake*. A member of the Ancaster family built an imitation sylvan retreat on it in 1835.

Montrose's army passed this way in 1645 during the Wars of the Covenant (the Civil War in England) when he attempted to win Scotland for Charles I, and when General Monk, Cromwell's hatchetman in Scotland, was trying to subdue the clans, a group of women and children took refuge on this island. A sergeant attempted to swim over and one of the Highland women, Helen Stewart, slashed his head off with a dirk when he emerged from the water.

This area is, of course, the heart of the Trossachs. The Wordsworths said they understood the name meant many hills. The woods were used for iron smelting and there is a persistent tradition that the Venetian sword-master, Andrew Ferrara, made some

of his famous swords here at the end of the sixteenth century.

Earlier, in 1611, the Privy Council were so incensed at the misbehaviour of the MacGregors that they ordered that all boats on Loch Lomond were to be transported overland to Loch Katrine and a punitive expedition launched. However, it fell through as the chiefs did not co-operate, and the MacGregors remained unscathed for the time being.

On the north side of the loch is Brenachoile, a house where Dr Archie Cameron, Lochiel's brother, was captured in March 1753 by Hanoverian soldiers when he returned to Scotland from France as part of a Jacobite plot. He was executed in London, being hanged, drawn and quartered, the last victim in Britain to so suffer.

A similar tradition is attached to Glen Buckie, Balquhidder: the answer would seem to imply that in these Jacobite glens Dr Cameron would be hidden in a series of 'safe houses'.

The area around Loch Katrine was once well populated, and the water level is higher than in past centuries. The remains of an old track can be seen in the woods opposite Ellen's Isle and high up on Ben A'n. The people transported bark and charcoal to Loch Achray.

Queen Victoria first visited here in October 1859 to open Glasgow's water supply from Loch Katrine, a mammoth scheme which did much to reduce disease in that industrial city.

Return from the top by the way you came or—if you

William and Dorothy Wordsworth visited Loch Katrine in 1803.

want a scramble in ancient woodland—go west until you are clear of the cliffs (you have got to be *sure* you are clear), then descend to the woods and walk and scramble your way back to the road on the north shore of Loch Katrine and then walk back to the pier and on to the car park.

Loch Katrine is pronounced Catrin. It has been suggested that the name derives from *ceiterein* (furies or fiends) or caterans (robbers), but derivations from girls' names (Catherine, Catriona) tend to be discounted.

The original Trossachs Hotel was a scruffy inn which stood on the knoll of Ardcheanachrochan (the height at the head of the knoll). Lord Willoughby d'Eresby built the new hotel in 1852 and additions were made from 1877 onwards.

Walks mainly

linked to Inversnaid

and Loch Lomond

Walk 33: Ben Lomond (3,192 feet), 2¾ miles from Rowardennan, east shore of Loch Lomond, via the B.827, Balmaha. O.S. sheet 56.

Ben Lomond is one of Scotland's best-known mountains and, possibly excluding Ben Nevis, the most frequently ascended. It is Scotland's most southerly Munro mountain.

The internationally known song, 'Loch Lomond' speaks of the steep, steep sides, but it can be climbed by easy gradients from Rowardennan and is regularly done so by families, youth clubs and hostellers. Its north side is steep and craggy and holds snow late in the year and its western Ptarmigan shoulder is also steep sided.

The famous song tells of the bonnie banks of Loch Lomond and indeed they are beautiful.

The song is thought to have its origin in the Jacobite garrison at Carlisle during the retreat north from Derby during the 1745 Rising. When the garrison surrendered many of the prisoners were executed.

INVERSNAID AND LOCH LOMOND

The song talks of the high road and the low road. The girl will make her own way back on foot and her lover, left behind, speaks of his soul taking 'the low road' back. However, there are other theories.

The derivation of Lomond is also the subject of several theories. Beinn Iaomainn, mountain of the beacon has been suggested. So has *leamh monadh*, elmwood mountain or a corruption of the Gaelic word *ioman*, meaning banner or shield.

From Rowardennan the route up and back is about five and a half miles and the ascent takes about three hours.

Being so near the Highland line there are outstanding views to both the Lowlands and the Southern Highlands. The views range from Tinto Hill in Lanarkshire, Stirling and the Forth estuary, the Firth of Clyde, Arran, Kintyre, Jura and Ben Nevis.

The famous tadpole-shaped loch is the biggest breach in the Highland Boundary Fault and, at twenty-seven and a half square miles, it is Britain's largest sheet of fresh water. The north end of its twenty-four-mile length is in the Highlands and its south end in the Lowlands.

It may once have been a sea loch—its foot is only four miles from sea water and the upper loch one and a half miles likewise. In the narrow upper sections it is 653 feet deep, one of the deepest lochs in Britain. The southern part is open and shallow.

The loch discharges into the Clyde estuary by the River Leven and, indeed, it was called Loch Leven before the thirteenth century. It is internationally known for wild life and also supplies over 200 million litres of water for industry each day.

INVERSNAID AND LOCH LOMOND

An old loch jingle speaks of a wave without a wind, a fish without a fin and a floating island, but the probable explanation is more prosaic: waves at the mouths of burns, eels and water weed 'rafts'.

Part of the south end is a national nature reserve and its ditches and river banks are the home of the Loch Lomond dock, the only place in Britain where this plant is found.

The east shore is beautifully wooded and alders were once used for clog making and for the production of charcoal which was used in the manufacture of gunpowder.

The oak woods are particularly beautiful. In past centuries they were regularly cropped for wood for houses and ships and they were also used for charcoal for iron smelting in local sites called 'bloomeries'. Oak-bark was also used for leather tanning.

The loch also contains an unusual fish, the powan, evolved from salmon-related ancestors trapped at the close of the last ice age.

Loch Lomond may be given park status by the local authorities, a controversial issue, and over 40,000 people are thought to visit it on a summer day and over two million each year. Swimming can be dangerous as the loch shelves and the water may be cold.

The southern end is island-dotted (the loch has about thirty in all) and most were inhabited in past centuries.

Nearly all can be seen from Ben Lomond or the walks in the following section—Conic Hill from its lower brow is particularly good—and the main ones include the following.

Inchcailloch: Isle of the women which once had a convent and church. St Kentigerna, mother of St Fillan, is believed to have died there in A.D. 734. Later, the church was the parish church of Buchanan parish and many Buchanans and MacGregors are buried there. *Cailleach* means an old woman and is a short form of *cailleach-dhubh*, a woman in black, a nun.

Inchmurrin: named after St Mirren, the patron saint of Paisley Abbey. The castle ruins were once the seat of the Earls of Lennox. Isabella, Duchess of Albany, is said to have retired here after her father, husband and two sons were executed by James I at Stirling (see Walk 28).

The islands are outwith the scope of this book but others worth mentioning are Clairinsh (the slogan of the Clan Buchanan), and Inchlonaig, off Luss, upon which Robert Bruce is said to have planted yews for his bowmen. The five islands stretching towards Inchmurrin from Balmaha—Creinch, Torrinch, Clairinsh, Aber Isle and Inchcailloch—form a nature reserve with part of the mainland shore of Endrick Water.

Most walkers ascend Ben Lomond from the Rowardennan car park and return the same way, but some mountaineers also go in from Gleann Dubh, off the B.829, a longish but attractive route, or from Comer Farm at the back of the Ben. The Comer road is private and permission is needed to take cars along it.

It is possible, too, to go in from Inversnaid by following the West Highland Way track to the Cailness Burn, then ascending on to the north ridge at around 1,500 feet between Cruinn a' Bheinn and the Ben. You can look down on the oddly named

Creag a' Bhocain (rock of the ghost). Care is needed on the final slopes to the summit, particularly in frosty conditions or in snow.

From Comer Farm, the ascent is steep and no place for the novice. Comer was the home of Gregor MacGregor, father of Rob Roy's wife.

A pleasant walk is to go in from the Loch Dhu car park (B.829, six miles from Aberfoyle) on the Forestry Commission's red route which goes over the shoulder of Ben Lomond to Rowardennan.

Gleann Dubh, Stronmacnair and Big and Little Bruach Caoruinn are all now swamped in trees but the remains of old dwellings and cultivation can be seen. Stronmacnair was also the site of a burial ground. *The New Statistical Account of Scotland* speaks of houses, cleared ground and a kiln for drying corn. At one time it would have been dotted with MacGregor townships.

It is about five miles to Rowardennan, but a good plan is to break off from the red route when near the Ben's south shoulder and go on to the summit from there by the tourist path.

It is possible to descend from the summit to Comer by going north to the dip between the Ben and Cruinn a' Bheinn and then going east down the long and lonely upper corrie. A deer fence has been erected in the corrie so a wide detour is needed to avoid it. Return by Gleann Dubh and Loch Dubh to the track and the B.829 Loch Dhu (different loch) car park. This round trip is about eighteen miles.

Alternatively, come back down from the summit to the Rowardennan shoulder and return to Loch Dhu the way you came.

When coming in from the B.829 and Loch Dhu you pass Loch Dhu House (see Walk 34, Loch Dhu and Loch Chon) and the Forestry Commission notice-board which gives the colours of various walks.

Follow the wide track. You will see a stone tower on the left which marks the buried pipe from Loch Katrine (see Walk 34, Loch Dhu and Loch Chon). The path is tree-bordered and you eventually pass a Nissen hut at a junction. Follow the red markers and pass an open space at the river where there is a bridge. Continue uphill and pass through a gate and a deer fence. As you gain height you pass an old, grey hut on the right. It is good for shelter in a squall but not much else.

It is tempting to cross the burn here because the track appears to end and there are stepping stones but do *not.* Stick to the north bank and the red markers start again soon. It quickly becomes an attractive moorland walk but *very* eroded and glaury (muddy), particularly after rain. You pass the remains of old shielings.

After leaving the trees (fence and stile) the route runs over wide moorland and then descends to Rowardennan. For Ben Lomond, leave the path at the crest of the moor at the point of your choice and head for the long shoulder of the Ben which carries the tourist track. You reach a pleasant burn and cross it. This is a beautiful walk in spring when the moorland birds are arriving or in summer when the heather is out (but there can be a problem with flies).

Either arrange two cars (one at Rowardennan, the other at Loch Dhu) or return to Loch Dhu the way you came.

Walk 34: Loch Dhu and Loch Chon, 6 miles there and back, B.829, way-marked woodland walk from Loch Dhu to the north end of Loch Chon. O.S. sheet 56.

This is very pleasant woodland walking but with limited views. For those interested in industrial archaeology, however, it has much of interest.

In the huge sweeps of forest between Loch Arklet and Aberfoyle the Forestry Commission have way-marked a network of inter-linked pleasant routes.

It is not possible to give all of these (see colour-guide on page 15), but some of the main ones give a taster.

This route needs a cautionary word because it is way-marked white on the Commission's boards and is signposted to Inversnaid.

But the path ends on the B.829 just north of Frenich Farm and if you want to go to Inversnaid you face another five and a half miles on a tarmac road which carries much tourist traffic. It is not therefore recommended as a route to Inversnaid.

Along this walk in secluded woods you see stone pillars, buttressed burn banks, iron foot-bridges, huge mausoleum-type towers with subterranean tunnels and large iron grills, all strongly constructed and fitting far better into the landscape than modern undressed concrete.

It is all in present-day use and forms part of one of the great engineering feats of the nineteenth century. Loch Katrine was chosen to be the main reservoir for Glasgow's water needs and its formal inauguration, on 20th May 1856, heralded a major step forward in the health of that great city. Loch Lubnaig, Strathyre and Balquhidder were all considered for this project but rejected.

Meall Meadhonach (middle-mound), separating Loch Katrine from the upper glen of Loch Chon, was pierced by a tunnel. Progress was often slow and at one stage only five yards a month were achieved, but it was all eventually crowned with success.

On 14th October 1859, Queen Victoria came with the Prince Consort and opened the sluices near the building on the south shore of Loch Katrine, now known as the Royal Cottage. Twenty-five years later another huge scheme got underway which was opened in 1901. The water in Loch Katrine was increased by water from Loch Arklet through a tunnel built in 1895.

The Loch Arklet dam was built between 1909 and 1914, and in 1919 the Loch Katrine level was again raised.

When you walk along the west side of Loch Chon you are seeing living memorials to major engineering feats.

Writer and mountaineer Tom Weir tells how, as a young boy, he walked out of Glasgow 'up the pipe track' to the Trossachs. Several small bothies (huts or shelters) had been built at the time of the pipe's construction. Here the hardy mountaineers and walkers who left the city in the Depression years and headed for the hills would find shelter for the night.

Further back in time, at Loch Ard, the MacGregors had a mill known as Mill of Chon, and also one at Inversnaid.

At the south end of Loch Dhu (the black loch), just past the road end going in to Loch Dhu House on your left, is a parking place with a litter-bin.

INVERSNAID AND LOCH LOMOND

Walk up towards the house and past a Forestry Commission notice which says 'Kinlochard, 4½ miles (blue), Milton, Aberfoyle, 6½ miles (yellow), Rowardennan, 7½ miles, via Ben Lomond at 1,200 feet (red)'.

Walk past Loch Dhu cottage and other buildings and at the right-hand side of the track-road you will see a notice, pointing right, into the trees, saying 'Path to Inversnaid, south side of Loch Chon'.

The path lips the side of the loch initially and passes through attractive woodland.

Soon you will see the markers (marked as towers on the map) of the buried pipeline and the other constructions.

You pass a series of dams, and at one you cross below it on a plank-bridge.

Near Frenich Farm, at the north-west end of Loch Chon (loch of the dogs or hounds) you temporarily emerge from the trees to a wide break and a gate. *Do not* go right. Cross the break and re-enter the trees by another break. To the right you can see the line of towers coming over from Loch Katrine, marking the tunnel through Meall Meadhonach. There is a marker on the trees at the left of the gate.

Not long after you pass near Frenich Farm you reach a large water-point with a fence right round it. On the left is a rickety wooden watch-tower.

Eventually the track widens and you reach a pole barrier and emerge on the road.

You can go on to Inversnaid if you wish, but it is better to return to Loch Dhu.

There are not many views on this walk, but it is a good one for appreciating the feats of the Victorian engineers.

Walk 35: Loch Dhu (B.829) to Kinlochard, 4½ miles, Forestry Commission way-marked walk (blue), very pleasant woodland walking. O.S. sheets 56 and 57.

Be wary of confusing the two black or dark lochs. Loch Dhu on map sheet 56 is beside the B.829 and at the south end of Loch Chon. Loch Dubh is in Gleann Dubh which runs north-west to Comer at the back of Ben Lomond. Loch Dhu is the one you want in this instance.

It might be helpful to read Walk 28, Loch Ard, Walk 33, Ben Lomond, and Walk 34, Loch Dhu and Loch Chon, before setting out on this one as they all have linking factors.

It follows the route for other Forestry Commission walks for part of the way with initial way-markers carrying chevrons of red, blue, yellow and white.

Blue is the colour you want.

It is probably best done from Loch Dhu to Kinlochard as, after an initial climb, you have a pleasant downhill tramp. You can easily walk back to your starting point after some refreshments in Kinlochard.

Loch Ard, of course, means the high loch and Kin is from the Gaelic word *ceann* (head).

Loch Ard was a hideaway for Murdoch, Duke of Albany, Earl of Fife and Earl of Menteith, in the thirteenth century. He succeeded his father as Regent of Scotland while James I of Scotland was captive for many years in England.

There is a structure on an island, Dun Dochil or Duke Murdoch's island, which he reputedly used as a bolt-hole. He was executed in 1425 for allegedly seeking to topple the throne.

Look out for attractive open and green sections beside the river which are pleasant places for a halt, a rest and something to eat.

En route you pass a dam and go through a gate and ultimately reach a baffling junction with a bridge going right to farm buildings. There are no markers at this junction but go *left* and you will pick them up.

You pass below a large viaduct which has had one pillar replaced or recoated in modern times and it is salutary to see the ugliness of concrete compared with the natural stone of the Victorian engineers.

At a four-way junction go *left*, and at another further on also go left and downhill. There are some small yellow notices on telegraph poles: these are *not* markers so ignore them.

Eventually the way-marked route to Aberfoyle (yellow) goes off right and you keep straight on (blue) and pass through gates and beside a series of houses until you strike the banks of Loch Ard. It is very attractive and lonely-looking at this point.

You pass the Loch Ard sailing club and reach the village. A Commission notice for way-marked walks says 'Aberfoyle, yellow, 7 miles—Drymen Road, brown, 8 miles—Cobleland, Gartmore, 7½ miles, pink/peach; Rowardennan, 8½ miles, Ben Lomond, red: Inversnaid, Frenich, 12 miles, white'.

(Remember, if you intend doing it, that this white route ends near Frenich Farm, over five miles from Inversnaid.)

Walk 36: Cruachan Hill (1,762 feet), 3 miles, hill-walk, between Loch Arklet (west end) and east shore of Loch Lomond. O.S. sheet 56.

If *you* want a short hill-walk with good views then take yourself up Cruachan Hill.

The name means a stack, in the sense of being heaped up, and it is a modest hill in comparison with its gigantic namesake Ben Cruachan at Loch Awe. But it is a fine viewpoint for some attractive corners.

(Ben Cruachan is more properly Cruachan Beinn, the heaped up hill of many peaks, and is the Clan Campbell war-cry or slogan.)

Our wee Cruachan is in totally MacGregor country.

Take the B.829 from Aberfoyle to the junction with the Stronachlachar road at the east end of Loch Arklet, then continue west on the road which ends at Inversnaid. Sections of this road are very old and partially follow old bridle tracks and the eighteenth-century military road.

Look out on the right of the road, not long after leaving Aberfoyle, for an old building marked on the map as The Teapot. It is now used as a byre, but it was once the site of illicit drinking. Following the Act of Union, stricter excise laws were applied to Scotland and whisky-making went underground. Illicit drinking was particularly prevalent during the nineteenth-century navvy work on the Loch Katrine pipeline. The still was hidden up the glen: strangers were given tea and friends were given something which looked like tea but was not. It was also a halt-place in the days of coaches and horses.

INVERSNAID AND LOCH LOMOND

About quarter of a mile past Garrison Farm, beyond Loch Arklet, is a secluded parking place on the south of the road and marked on the map.

You drive across a wooden bridge over the burn. There are seats in the park.

All the hills across Loch Lomond are clearly seen, but the loch itself is hidden by folds in the ground.

Ben Vorlich is easily identified by the North of Scotland Hydro Electric Board's pipes coming out of its side and steep-sided Ben Vane (the middle mountain) lies behind the once beautiful Coiregrogain, now sprinkled with hydro installations.

To the south of Ben Vane is A'Chrois and Creag Tharsuinn (cross-grained crag) with flat-topped Beinn Narnain behind.

The car park was constructed by 53 Field Squadron of the Royal Engineers in 1966. A path at the back of the car park leads to a gate which takes you on to the hillside. Move left (east) to follow the burn and gradually Loch Lomond and the houses and caravans of Inveruglas on the far shore come into view.

There lay the MacFarlane lands, not a large clan but a tough one. People long ago called the moon MacFarlane's Lantern because of their cattle-reiving habits.

It was said that they paid their daughters' tochers by the light of the Michaelmas Moon; that is, they gave their daughters a wedding dowry as a result of their cattle raids in September when the moonlit night gave enough light to see by and enough dark for concealment.

Follow a fence steeply uphill, and the view widens. Loch Long and the Arrochar Hills appear, upper Loch

Lomond opens up, Ben Venue is easily recognised, and the waters of Loch Arklet and Loch Katrine spread out below.

Across the way, Garrison Farm stands on its knoll with the tiny schoolhouse nearby. This was originally an eighteenth-century military fort built to control the passes in a bid to curb the turbulent MacGregors. It was burned by them in the 1745 Jacobite Rising. General Wolfe, who won the Heights of Abraham against Montcalm's French in the conquest of Canada, served there for a time. The fort was provisioned by boat to Inversnaid.

Steep-sided Creag an Fhithich beside the Loch Lomond shore becomes prominent and so do the attractive hills beyond Garrison Farm, Beinn a' Choin, Stob-an Fhàinne and Maol Mór.

The fence takes a sharp bend and then goes over the top of the hill. There is a small cairn and excellent views are to be had.

Good views can be had, too, to scenery which may well change in the future. That is, the north-west corries of Ben Lomond. This side of the Ben will hold a reservoir if the Hydro Board's plans for Europe's biggest pumped storage (Craigrostan) scheme on the Ben come to fruition.

Tiny Lochan Cruachan just down from the top is worth a visit and there are pleasant views into lonely Gleann Gaoithe which leads to Comer at the back of the Ben.

Loch Arklet, now a reservoir, takes on a natural look with height and it is difficult to realise, looking at the empty landscape, that on 27th September 1715, over three hundred MacGregors paraded here and were reviewed by three MacGregor leaders, Glen

Gyle, Rob Roy and Balhaldie, and then created havoc in the lands of hostile families and clans.

In the little modern church at Loch Arklet there is a stained glass window commemorating the MacGregors of Corriearklet.

Return the way you came or, if you are sure-footed on steep ground, pick a careful way down the rocky front of the hill to the banks of Loch Lomond. You will probably see the ruins of old MacGregor homesteads. One such, on a knoll, has a marvellous view down Loch Lomond. At the lochside take the West Highland Way track to Inversnaid, then take the road back up to the car park. This road is steep and busy in summer, therefore take care, and walk facing on-coming traffic.

Walk 37: Maol Mór (2,223 feet), Beinn a' Choin (2,499 feet) and Stob-an Fhàinne (2,121 feet), 6½ miles, hill-walk, north-west of Stronachlachar, Loch Katrine. O.S. sheet 56.

These moundy, rough hills bounded by Glen Gyle to the north-east and Loch Arklet to the south, can give the true flavour of the MacGregor hills.

They are rarely visited and to get on to Maol Mór (big mound) one should apply for permission because it means crossing water-board ground when leaving Stronachlachar. Glen Gyle forms the upper end of Strath Gartney which, nineteen miles long, splits the Trossachs from Callander to the hills at the head of Loch Lomond.

INVERSNAID AND LOCH LOMOND

Park at the pier and walk back up past the large house (right) and then turn sharp right with other houses on your left.

Pass through a green gate at the left of the road and cross soft and marshy ground to a fence. The lower strand permits you to go under without disturbing it. Climb steeply up the hillside to where two trees (one dead) make prominent markers. A faint track can be found but in summer the bracken makes heavy going.

It is worth pausing to look back at Stronachlachar below, Loch Katrine stretching out and the island, now covered in rhododendrons and buttressed all round, where Rob Roy marooned Graham of Killearn, the Duke of Montrose's factor and kinsman. He was seized near Aberfoyle and relieved of the rents he had just collected. He was later released, a fortunate man because he had burned Rob's house and evicted his family.

Continue steeply uphill over knolls and strike a fence which takes the easiest line over a wide bowl.

Maol Mór is a *very* knolly and rough hill.

Eventually, you top the highest mound where there is a trig point.

The view is magnificent: Ben Lomond across the way, Ben Venue, Ben Ledi, Stuc a' Chroin and Ben Vorlich, Ben More and Stob Binnein, Beinn Tulaichean and Cruach Ardrain, Dumyat and the Ochils, a spectacular view of Ben Lui (Laoigh) and its neighbours Ben Oss and Ben Dubhchraig, and Beinn Ime, Beinn Narnain and the other Ben Vorlich at Arrochar and Loch Lomond.

Glen Gyle stretches out and the cattle route over the Parlan Pass to Inverarnan becomes clear—at Lag a' Chuirn, on the slopes of Ben Ducteach, huts once stood, known as Tigh na Cuirte, the 'court-house', where cattle thieves were tried.

The Bealach nan Corp is across the way.

It is more rough walking to reach Beinn a' Choin (mountain of the dogs or hounds), and it is useful to remember that a fence connects it and Stob-an Fhàinne (peak of the Fianne, mythical warriors).

There is only a tiny cairn on Stob-an Fhàinne. Just beyond the top there is an excellent view of the isthmus which connects the sea loch of Loch Long and Loch Lomond. It is only 100 feet above sea level. You can see the houses of the modern village of Tarbet. The Gaelic name *Tarbet* means a boat-drag but has come to be applied to any isthmus.

Some of the Norsemen of King Haakon took this route in 1263 after they gathered in the Clyde to try and assert Norse authority over western Scotland and the Hebrides. The Scots king, Alexander III, was only twenty-two but sagely dragged out negotiations in the hope that winter storms would imperil the Norsemen.

The exasperated invaders sent about forty longships up Loch Long to Arrochar, dragged them over to Loch Lomond, sailed down the loch and sacked the settlements of Lennox. However, the Norsemen got their come-uppance because they were to be decisively defeated at the Battle of Largs.

Once you leave the hill-top look out for a break in the cliffs on the left which will take you down towards the Corriearklet Burn although you have to detour to the right at one stage before you get right down to where a very marshy vehicle track runs down the glen.

When getting near the Loch Arklet road keep to the right (west) of the houses and a green corrugated-iron steading and a white, roadside building. A fence which initially runs across the hillside turns sharply down to the road. Follow it down on its outside. The roadside fence can be crossed below the lower strand without touching the posts or the wires. Walk back up the road to Stronachlachar.

In Dorothy Wordsworth's day the loch was a 'small tarn', but it is now a large reservoir. It is hard for us to understand nowadays that in past centuries about one hundred and fifty people lived between here and Inversnaid.

Before the road was made thirty ponies were kept near Stronachlachar to take people from the Loch Katrine boat to Inversnaid.

Corriearklet Farm was where Rob Roy married Mary of Comer at New Year in 1693.

This is a hill-walk for the fit. Stay clear at stalking and lambing times.

Walk 38: The Parlan Hill Pass, 8 miles, hill-walk, Inverarnan, Glen Falloch, Loch Lomond (A.82) to Glen Gyle (Stronachlachar), Loch Katrine (or vice versa). O.S. sheet 56.

The Glen Gyle MacGregors and Rob Roy, in particular, used this pass to reach the old droving inn at Inverarnan, to get into Glen Falloch, and also—on occasion— to push west into Argyll. It is also the route the cattle-drovers took from Glen Falloch to Loch Katrineside. (Rob Roy for a time had a house, under Campbell protection, at the head of Glen Shira, near Inveraray, when his own dwellings in Glen Gyle and Craigrostan were burned by his enemies.)

This fine stretch of lonely hill country, flanked by beautiful mountains and linking with the Bealach nan Corp route to Inverlochlarig and Balquhidder, is nowadays scenically marred by a line of pylons but the wildness of the landscape at several points even dominates and loses these. The Hydro Board engineers have understandably used the pass for the transmission line to and from the pumped storage scheme at Cruachan, Loch Awe.

It is normally excellent country for seeing deer (but avoid it in the stalking season).

James Hogg, the Ettrick Shepherd, also took this route in the nineteenth century while herding sheep. *Parlan* is the Gaelic for Bartholomew and the hill itself has ancient associations.

The MacFarlanes, whose lands mainly lay around Loch Sloy and on the west side of Loch Lomond, and into Glen Falloch, were heirs male of the twelfth-century Celtic Earls of Lennox through their ancestor Parlan who is commemorated in this hill. They were later displaced by the Darnley Stewarts.

The hill has a squarish rocky top, has a fey feeling and—a rare event nowadays—no cairn.

An enjoyable two-car expedition is for one party to drive to Stronachlachar on the B.829, leave the car there and walk on the private metalled road on the north-west bank of the long arm of Loch Katrine and up the Glen Gyle Water below the crags of Ben Ducteach. A court-house for cattle thieves once stood here. (The other car goes to Inverarnan.) The pylons are unmistakable markers.

You have to cross some tributary burns so take great care when the burns are swollen by melting snow or prolonged rain.

Two and a half miles from the head of the loch and at the north end of Ben Ducteach the crest of the pass is reached at 1,800 feet and is easily identified by a fence (now the boundary between Strathclyde and Central Regions) and a small lochan.

The line of pylons below you and swinging east gets lost in the boggy, heathery flats leading down to the Ben Glas (green mountain) Burn.

If you have included Parlan Hill you can easily descend north from it to Lochan Beinn Chabhair (pronounced Ch-abar with 'ch' as in loch), the small loch of the mountain of the antler, which lies below the fine 3,053-foot mountain of that name.

From there follow the Ben Glas Burn down to Inverarnan. There is an intermittent path, on the north bank, which is well defined in its lower sections.

The views from Parlan Hill are very attractive, with Loch Lomond looking secluded and the long glen to Inverlochlarig, Balquhidder, looking much as it has done for centuries.

One January, while sitting at the crest of the pass and before going up the hill, I and others saw a small burn near the top being caught by the wind as it poured over some rocks and held upright in a geyser-like pillar for minutes on end.

To follow the true line of the ancient pass-route descend north-west from the Parlan Pass lochan and plod across the moor. A burn with narrow sections and large pools links with the Ben Glas Burn.

INVERSNAID AND LOCH LOMOND

The path on the north bank of the Ben Glas Burn needs care when it drops steeply down to Ben Glas Farm near the A.82 (T) road.

It can be greasy in wet weather but the steep slope is zig-zagged to make the gradient easier.

In snow or ice conditions the greatest care must be taken as here and there the path lips the burn-gorge and the magnificent, white, splayed-out waterfall which can be seen so prominently above Ben Glas Farm from the Loch Lomond road.

As you near the farm wall and fence, go left (as you face the farm) and you will find a stile. You then see the West Highland Way signs, cross another stile and by being routed slightly west and then north you curve round to reach the banks of the River Falloch and its bridge which leads you to the road. The pleasant inn at Inverarnan lies a few hundred yards southwards down the road.

The ruin you see near the farm is the former farm building. In wet weather the river frequently overflows and these flats are often under water so be prepared to paddle on occasion.

A short canal-like section was formerly a channel dug in the nineteenth century to let tourist boats on Loch Lomond bring their passengers right up to the hotel.

If you do not fancy a two-car expedition, one at Stronachlachar and the other at Inverarnan and exchanging keys in mid-moor, then a pleasant round walk which is not a pass-crossing but which gives the flavour, is to start from Inverarnan and walk to the crest of the Parlan Pass, take in Parlan Hill, and return by Lochan Beinn Chabhair and the Ben Glas Burn.

INVERSNAID AND LOCH LOMOND

For that, walk up to the bridge past Ben Glas Farm, cross the river, and follow the West Highland Way signs until you see the stile routing people south on the West Highland Way. Cross that stile (do not go to the stile at the farm wall and fence at the back) and a tiny path which disappears every now and again goes steeply eastwards up the south bank of the Ben Glas Burn. If you lose it, do not worry. Just keep plodding upwards until the first steep section is over. You will understand why the drovers in the seventeenth, eighteenth and nineteenth centuries took their cattle up the zig-zags on the other bank but even there, and at a slow pace, they must have lost much weight.

However, the south bank gives magnificent close-up views of the falls. When on the moor, ignore the pylons if you can, cross the moor and head for the obvious 'dip' of the pass where the pylons cross it. Once on top of the pass ascend Parlan Hill, descend to Lochan Beinn Chabhair and return by the other bank to Inverarnan.

Inverarnan is an excellent place in which to have a drink and is popular with mountaineers, walkers and passing skiers.

In past centuries the north end of Loch Lomond was the meeting-place for three drovers' routes, and the inn itself was on the route from Argyll. Some went north to Glen Dochart and on to Crieff, and others went down to Loch Lomondside.

From Glen Gyle and Loch Katrine the cattle were driven to Aberfoyle, crossed the flat ground at the head of the Forth, came by Gartmoren into the valley of the Endrick Water and on to the big fairs at Falkirk where many were bought by English dealers.

During the 1719 Jacobite Rising Rob Roy and fifty MacGregors attacked a posse of soldiers at Inverarnan, killing one, wounding others and disarming all. A £200 reward and a free pardon for any outlaw who captured Rob Roy was speedily announced but without any takers.

The inn later became a popular hotel. Visitors included Nathaniel Hawthorne in 1857 who had a wet day of a 'Scotch mist' of an all too familiar kind.

The next two walks pose problems for the writer because they are both part of the statutory Long Distance Footpath, the West Highland Way, which runs ninety-five miles from Milngavie to Fort William. Erosion is bad and continuing visitor pressure a serious problem. This section is now so well-known that to omit it from the book would be odd, to say the least, yet to include it compounds the problem.

Many people get immense pleasure from the beautiful sections between Rowardennan and Inversnaid and between Inversnaid and Inverarnan. Others feel that poles, signs, bridges, rock steps and walk-ways have harmed the wilderness quality. The debate continues.

Much of the Rowardennan section is a tough forestry road but the woodland paths are now greatly affected by erosion.

Each walker should think twice before embarking on them at all. The decision is yours.

Walk 39: Rowardennan to Inversnaid (or vice versa), 7 miles, by the shores of Loch Lomond. O.S. sheet 56.

This is a route of great antiquity, passing through the lands of the MacGregors, with magnificent views at the Inversnaid end across Loch Lomond to the so-called 'Arrochar Alps'.

The route passes below Ben Lomond and its lower offshoot of Craigrostan, once part of the personal estate of Rob Roy and—at the time of writing—the proposed site of a North of Scotland Hydro Electric Board giant pump storage project which involves buildings and installations at the water's edge and a high-level dam in Ben Lomond's hitherto unspoiled northern corries.

There is a choice of route at certain points, either a winding track through the old woods near the shore or a Forestry Commission road higher up which gives good views at some points but is duller walking. Take the road as the paths are very eroded. It is way-marked by the Forestry Commission and is part of the West Highland Way.

Sections of the lower path are very unpleasant in bad weather as the ground is glaury (muddy).

For those organising two parties and one car at either end, and exchanging keys midway, it should be stressed that the drive from Aberfoyle to Inversnaid (B.829) is one of the most beautiful in the country and itself follows ancient routes.

The lochside path was used by the MacGregors after excursions into the Lowlands.

Each walker will have his own preference, but the route is perhaps best begun from the Rowardennan end. When you drive there from Drymen (B.837) you are leaving the lands of the Clan Buchanan and passing through the famous Pass of Balmaha, another route familiar to the MacGregors.

The name Rowardennan (your starting point) is derived from *Rudha Aird Eanain*, point of the height of Adamnan, the biographer of St Columba. Eanan is from *Adhamhan*, little Adam.

There are fine pines here in an attractively secluded Forestry Commission parking site.

Long ago a ferry operated between Rowardennan and Inverbeg (and still operates: check locally) and cattle herds were swum across the loch.

When walking from Rowardennan, the Forestry Commission's indicator board is at the back beside the toilet block. The signs are 'Rowardennan, red; Kinlochard, blue; Inversnaid, white'.

Go left, and you will soon see white discs and the thistle-sign of the poles of the West Highland Way.

You pass a signpost which says 'Inversnaid, seven miles'.

Go past the youth hostel, then Rowchmock youth campsite (left), which is run by the Forestry Commission.

There is a good view (right) to Ptarmigan Hill and you are now walking on a broad forest 'road'. You pass the entrance to Ptarmigan Lodge. (A ptarmigan is a white mountain 'grouse'.) About one hundred yards on, you pass through an iron gate and later reach a sign which points (left) down made-up steps to the lower woodland path. Stick to the Forestry Commission road (upper) which is easier walking and which avoids erosion.

Look out (left) for good views of the Cobbler and Beinn Narnain.

Farther on, watch out (left) for a large, flattish cairn and a footpath through the trees to the edge of a cliff. There are attractive views of the islands and below are the remains of MacGregor homesteads. Take care because the rocks can be slippy.

Back on the track, you come to a junction. Take the high (right) path. It goes uphill, then curves down to the loch again.

The forest road ends at a 'Fire' sign and a small path continues on.

The upper track 'misses' Rowchoish bothy which stands near the lower woodland track. The lower track and the forest road are linked by a junction track not long before the bothy, and the two come together past the bothy. It was once part of a township that as late as 1759 contained homes for nine families.

This bothy is now named the William Ferris Memorial shelter, after a prominent Scottish walker, and has been restored by the Scottish Rights of Way Society. At the time of writing, it has no door or window glass and is no more than a storm shelter in bad weather. William Ferris was founder of the Rucksack Club, from which the S.Y.H.A. evolved. He founded the Scottish Ramblers Federation, and was chairman and director of the Rights of Way Society.

The name Rowchoish means *Rudha a' Choin*, point of the hollow. Your route crosses a deer fence (stile) and there is a foot-bridge over the burn at the next house, the sheep farm of Cailness (*Croill Innis*, wood of the recess, i.e. sheltered).

The track rolls on, with intriguing views of the Arrochar Hills, and crosses some awful erosion and some awkward sections (one has an unforgivable banister wire inserted through three trees).

The arrival at Inversnaid is dramatic. The name is derived from *inbhir* (estuary or mouth) and *sna'thaid* (the needle, the name of a burn).

Here there is a large roaring waterfall, a large hotel, and a small harbour now used as a base for pleasure craft but which was once of importance in the past when long lochs like Loch Lomond were main transport routes. The waterfall is smaller now with water being diverted to Loch Arklet.

Many a punitive operation has landed at Inversnaid in vain pursuit of the MacGregors. (Rob Roy had a ledge below the path, near Ptarmigan Lodge, to which prisoners were lowered on a rope.) His house was burned by Campbell of Killearn in 1712 and his family was evicted.

The busy west-bank Loch Lomond road is only a mile away across the water but (other than the hotel ferry boat) you would have to make a fifty-five mile detour to get there.

About a mile further north (see the following section), there is a cave reputedly used by Rob Roy and, in the fourteenth century, by King Robert the Bruce when he was a fugitive in the Scottish Wars of Independence.

It is said that when he was hidden in the cave wild goats lay down at the entrance. Bruce's pursuers passed by, thinking the cave was empty. Later, Bruce is reputed to have made a decree marking an area near Inversnaid as a goat sanctuary.

You can sometimes see modern descendants of these goats when walking the Rowardennan–Inversnaid route.

The view to the hills across the loch is magnificent —to A'Chrois, Beinn Ime, Ben Vane and Ben Vorlich.

It is marred only by the hydro pipes on the sides of Ben Vorlich, an essential project that is an unnecessary eyesore and, if mooted now, would probably be undergrounded or trenched and camouflaged by trees.

There have been suggestions, some as early as 1841 by the minister of Buchanan parish in *The New Statistical Account of Scotland*, that a road be pushed through from Rowardennan to Inversnaid. This was also proposed as relief work for the unemployed during the 1930s by Tom Johnston, later Secretary of State for Scotland.

The Wordsworths and Coleridge visited Inversnaid and praised the beauty and gaiety of the local people, and William wrote his poem 'The Highland Girl' about the ferryman's daughter. Another literary visitor was Nathaniel Hawthorne in 1857.

The Jesuit poet, Gerard Manley Hopkins, also visited this hamlet, and his prophetic poem on wilderness, entitled 'Inversnaid', was greatly influenced by his time there:

> What would the world be, once bereft
> Of wet and of wildness? Let them be left,
> O let them be left, wildness and wet;
> Long live the weeds and the wilderness yet.

I leave it to the reader and walker to decide whether his plea is being answered or not.

A herd of goats helped save the fugitive King Robert the Bruce.

Walk 40: Inversnaid to Inverarnan A.82 (T), 6½ miles, lochside walk, rough going in sections. O.S. sheet 56.

This is part of the West Highland Way and judged to be the most rough section, but there are buttressed steps, bridges, walk-ways with rails, chiselled hand- and footholds on boulders, and way-markers.

The path is heavily eroded.

Opposite Ardlui there is a signal which you can hoist, and a ferry will come over for you on a cash-and-carry basis if you want to leave the walk at that point.

Nathaniel Hawthorne said of this stretch of Loch Lomond, in front of Inversnaid, that 'It was the most beautiful lake and mountain view that I have ever seen'.

This writer has not too much enthusiasm for this walk since it was 'tamed' and made artificial, but it is undoubtedly beautiful.

A mile north of Inversnaid Hotel there is a mass of huge boulders and bluffs, Sròn Uaidh, which contains a cavern reputed to have been a shelter used by King Robert the Bruce when he was a fugitive after his defeats at Methven and Dalrigh during the Scottish Wars of Independence. The goats incident described previously is said to have taken place here.

Rob Roy is also reputed to have used it, and it is called Rob Roy's Cave on the map.

Dorothy Wordsworth visited it twice: in 1803 with her brother and Coleridge, and in 1822 accompanied by a party from a steamer.

It is quite hard to find, and some outdoor vandal has painted 'cave' on the rocks.

You tramp through woods and along the rough hillside and pass the remains of crofts at Pollochro, below Creag an Fhithich. Offshore you will see the oddly-named Island I Vow, a corruption of a lost Gaelic name starting with *Eilean* (island) and the rest a jumble. It may be *eilean buidhe* (pronounced booee), yellow island.

At Doune there is a restored, unlocked bothy, which provides good shelter.

The path runs past Ardleish, over a mound past the Dubh Lochan and down to the flats at Belnglas Farm where you can cross the Falloch River and get on to the A.82 (T). Inverarnan Hotel is just down the road and a good place to be picked up from.

Walk 41: Conic Hill (1,175 feet), 2 miles, hill-walk, Balmaha, Loch Lomond, B.827. O.S. sheet 56.

The south-east corner of Loch Lomond contains several attractive walks and the steep mound of Conic Hill particularly draws the eye.

The name probably derives from *A'chòinneach*, the moss or bog, and to the north and east lies rough moorland.

It is a splendid viewpoint and a geologically interesting boundary hill because it is part of the resistant edges of Lowland strata which have been pushed steeply up by the Highland Boundary Fault line.

As well as the loch's many islands you can also see the tower block flats of Glasgow.

It looks down on the mouth of the River Endrick and the marshes there form part of the Loch Lomond nature reserve.

Balmaha Pass is the key to the east shore and even the modern road does not entirely hide the strategic importance of this corner. It was a regular MacGregor route to and from the Lowlands.

The origin of the name is uncertain but it may derive from St Maha or Mahew, a shadowy figure from the Celtic Church era. Bal is from *baile*, a township.

In the Depression years—the hungry thirties—hardy city-born mountaineers walked, cycled or hitched to reach this area. Some used to catch late-night buses from Glasgow to Balmaha, row fourteen miles up the loch to Tarbet, walk through to Arrochar, climb on the Cobbler or Beinn Narnain or the other hills there, and return the same way. They slept out in makeshift shelters or in caves. It was not only the old MacGregors who were tough.

The statutory Long Distance Footpath, the West Highland Way, runs along the side of Conic Hill.

To climb Conic Hill, drive to the prominent car park at Balmaha at the right (north) of the road. There are toilets and a notice-board. Go to the back of the park where two way-marked walks, described later, are also indicated.

The path is clearly seen. You pass a notice for West Highland Way walkers which says: 'Lambing and calving, April and May, high route closed, walkers advised to take low route, Garadhban Forest via main road to Milton of Buchanan'.

To gain the hill, go up through the pleasant woods of mature pine, larch and spruce, of the Garadhban forest.

A junction path goes steeply uphill. Take that. It is not the Way route which is a few yards further on, but it also goes up, left, into a gap between the knolls.

The first hillock alone is worth going on to: you see the Gargunnock Hills, Fintry Hills, the gap to Bearsden, the Campsies and Duncryne, the Endrick estuary and most of the Loch Lomond islands, Inveruglas and the Luss Hills, the Arrochar Hills, Ben Lomond and the Ptarmigan shoulder.

If you want to continue to the top of Conic Hill, you face a slight drop down. The Way track, which you follow, runs to the left (north-west) of the Conic ridge and takes you to the back, from which the main top is easily reached. Alternatively, go straight up the knolls. There is also a path but it gets scrambly here and there.

When you are on the summit the front knoll hides part of the loch view.

It is not advisable to descend the long south-west ridge as that means returning to the car park along the busy road.

If you leave from this side, however, you cross a stile beside an iron gate opposite another car park, and go up through trees until the track reaches transmission line poles, with a thick half-pole at the side. A small track, partly hidden, goes right, and then steeply uphill and along the ridge to the gap where the Way comes in.

Those uncertain of navigation should go up and down from the main Balmaha car park.

Walk 42: Balmaha forest walks. O.S. sheet 56.

These walks start from the same car park as for Conic Hill.

There is a sign at the back which indicates white and blue way-marked routes.

White takes you uphill and is for the nimble. Blue is a gentle stroll.

Some of the white marking is mystifying so prepare to be adventurous.

Following the white markers you pass a tiny lochan and then go uphill through fine woods. An early seat gives views to the Campsies, to Gartocharn, the Endrick estuary and the islands. There are many fine larches. The path swings left and you see an excellent holly.

Keep a good look out because markers are few as the path rises steeply and then goes right and up. You emerge on a patch of conglomerate rock, moss-covered and with good views. Beware of the edge.

Cast around for markers and go straight ahead, keeping the gap on the right and you will see another marker.

You work back to a second gap through pleasant trees and glimpses of Conic Hill (on your right) with a marker to the left.

There is a mystifying double-back on the top of the knoll and, as you descend off it, watch out for three prominent downed trees heaped together. You go to another knoll where there is a plank seat overlooking the loch.

Look for a faint track downhill and after a bit you will find a marker which brings you back to the first knoll and the gap with the seat. There are fine views across the loch.

Descending further downhill you will find a steep section, with a wooden banister beside a gigantic Scots pine. The path splits, but both sections take you down to the road where there is a stile. Follow the road back to the Balmaha car park but be careful of traffic.

For the blue low-level walk, go through the gate at the back of the car park. A gentle walk along paths follows, through trees, across some foot-bridges, and then returns to the road and back to the car park. It is suitable for a family and dog.

Walk 43: Sallochy wood walks, Loch Lomond, 3½ miles north of Balmaha, off the B.837. O.S. sheet 56.

The Forestry Commission have some way-marked walks by the lochside. The high-level walk (one and a half miles) is one of the most pleasant and has two variations. There is another walk at the shore.

Watch out for a signposted car park to the left of the road.

Once you park you have to walk *back* to the road and cross it to the eastern side.

The path goes steeply uphill beside telegraph power poles and you will come across some benches. Turn right there. The path is marked with white discs, and some of the trees have name tags on them.

The path leads you to the moss-covered ruined

walls of the old township of Sallochy, an evocative spot, and then crosses a forest road. At a mystifying junction do not go right but follow the telegraph poles just where the stone 'spill' can be seen.

Height gauges for forestry lorries are beside you on the forest road but when you get to the 'spill' turn right. At a junction blue markers take you to a viewpoint and white take you back to the car park.

If you are going to the viewpoint the going is slightly rough and you have to cross two burns. You pass a seat, and when you reach the viewpoint the panorama of the loch is magnificent. It is rocky so take care when there and also when you are turning back to the path.

This is a walk for an energetic family or for savouring the feel of the bonny banks. The woods have housed quarriers, iron smelters, the clansmen of old, and 'crofters'. The name Sallochy is derived from the Gaelic *seileach* (willow).

On the loch side of the road a sign at the shore says: 'Forestry Commission Barbecue Site, by arrangement with the head forester (Drymen 255). Toilet facilities at Rowardennan'.

The bay-shore walk coincides with part of the West Highland Way and is badly eroded with much water lying in puddles if you walk it after rain.

To find the way-marked shore walk it is tempting to go north to the barbecue site and beyond, but in fact it goes south from the shore at the edge of the car park.

At the time of writing the way-markers (white) are poor and vanish after a time. This is very pleasant deciduous woodland of a type sadly vanishing from Scotland and it is pleasant to wander around and make you own way back to the car park. With the loch to the west and the road to the east it is difficult to go far wrong.

This park and bay are very popular in the summer.

Walk 44: Lochside stroll. O.S. sheet 56.

As you drive from Balmaha towards Rowardennan watch out for the Forestry Commission boundary sign at the left of the road, about one and a half miles from Balmaha.

Turn left *immediately at the sign* into a small clearing.

A way-marked path (white markers) takes you down to the shore, passing some boat-huts and crossing an askew bridge.

When walking parallel to the loch watch out for your junction path back which has no way-marker at the corner. It swings off sharply right at a large oak tree and the markers reappear once you are walking along it.

If you go past the junction you will strike a large burn and have to pick your own way back to the road.

This track can be very muddy in wet weather and is busy in the summer.

Try it out of season. On one stroll I saw jays, carrion-crows, a heron, two mallard, coal, blue and great tits, a robin, some redwings and two roe-deer. But that was November.

A short and pleasant walk for the strolling family or the car driver who wants to stretch his legs.

NOTES